Make your own handicraft gifts

Acknowledgments:

The publishers would like to thank the following:

David Constable, Candle Makers Supplies, 4 Beaconsfield Terrace Road, London W14 for supplying the candles

Dylon International Limited for tie-dyed and fabric painted articles

Gover Grey Photography for taking the photographs

Frontispiece: A selection of handicraft gifts, including knitting, decorating china, candlemaking, fabric painting, embroidery, fabric craft, beadwork

First published in 1975 by
Octopus Books Limited
59 Grosvenor Street, London W.1.

ISBN 0 7064 0350 9

Distributed in U.S.A. by
Crescent Books, a division of Crown Publishers Inc
419 Park Avenue South, New York, N.Y. 10016

Printed by Mandarin Publishers Limited
14 Westlands Road, Quarry Bay, Hong Kong
Printed in Hong Kong

Make your own Handicraft Gifts

by Sheila Richardson
and Eve Harlow

Octopus Books

Contents

Abbreviations

Knitting

alt	alternate
beg	begin (ning)
c4L	Cable 4 left. Slip next 2 sts on to cable needle and hold at front of work, k2, then k2 from cable needle
c4R	Cable 4 right. Sl next 2 sts on to cable needle and hold at back of work, k2 from left-hand needle, k2 from cable needle
cm	centimetre
cn	cable needle
dec	decrease
fin	finish (ing)
g-st	garter st (every row k)
inc	increase (ing)
k	knit
m 1	make 1 st by putting yarn over or round needle
p	purl
patt	pattern
psso	pass slipped st over
pick 1 k	pick up one st from row below and k it
rem	remain (ing)
rep	repeat
sl	slip
st(s)	stitch (es)
st-st	stocking stitch (1 row k, 1 row p)
tog	together
tbl	through back of loop
Twist 3R	sl next 2 sts on to right-hand needle, sl next st on to cable needle and hold at front of work, return 2 sts to right-hand needle, k st from cable needle, k 2
Twist 3L	sl next st on to cable needle and hold at front of work, k 2, k 1 from cable needle

Crochet

ch	chain
dc (sc)	double crochet (single crochet)
sl-st	slip stitch
tr	treble

Note

Where terms or materials differ for overseas readers an equivalent is given in parenthesis after the British term or material.

Patchwork

Patchwork is one of the most delightful crafts in the world and, if you like fine sewing, you will love patchwork. Although there are dozens of exciting patchwork patterns on record and most of them originated by the early American settler women, if you are just a beginner, you will want to try an easy pattern first. Next to the square, the pentagon shape is the simplest to work with because the angles are wide which makes joining up easier. The patchwork pig and the perfumed ball are all made with pentagon shapes and the stuffed cat is made up of square and rectangular patches stitched together at random.

Perfume ball

illustrated on page 11

Materials
Scraps of cotton or silk fabric in toning colours and matching patterns ($\frac{1}{4}$ yard of each of six different fabrics will make about 20 perfume balls).
Matching thread
Stiff paper for backing
Stiff card for templates
Loose lavender or potpourri
2 yards satin baby ribbon
Sharp knife
Ruler with metal edge
Pencil
Protractor

Preparing for patchwork The shape used here is a pentagon, a five-sided shape. You can trace off the pentagon shapes given here to make templates or, for greater accuracy, draw your own. The more accurate your template, the

better your finished patchwork. Two templates are required for patchwork – one is used for cutting out the fabric pieces and the other is used to cut out backing papers. To make the perfume ball illustrated, the fabric template measures $1\frac{1}{2}$ inches along each side of the shape and includes $\frac{1}{4}$ inch turnings. The backing template measures 1 inch along each of the sides.

Fabric template Draw a horizontal line exactly $1\frac{1}{2}$ inches long. Place the protractor so that the 90 degrees line is exactly on the left end of the line and mark with a pencil dot the angle of 72 degrees (diagram 1). Join the dot and the

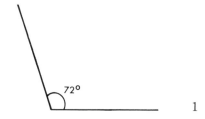

1

left side of the horizontal line and make this line exactly $1\frac{1}{2}$ inches long. Turn the card and place the 90 degree line of the protractor on the end of the line and again mark 72 degrees (diagram 2).

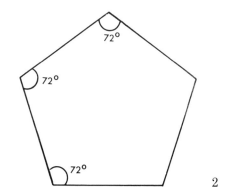

2

Continue, always working on the left side of the line and to the left and making the line 1½ inches long. Thus you will draw a pentagon shape. Cut out the completed shape very carefully with a very sharp pointed knife and using a metal edged rule.

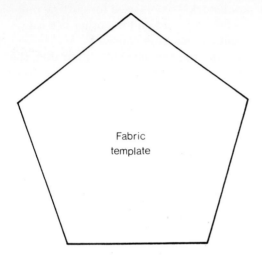

Fabric
template

Backing template Draw a pentagon as above but make each line 1 inch long. Cut the template out of stiff card.

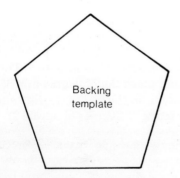

Backing
template

Cutting out fabrics and backing papers Press all the creases out of the fabrics and lay them on a flat surface. Place the template on the wrong side of the fabric and draw round the shape with a sharply pointed soft pencil. Cut out 12 pentagon shapes, two from each

of six different fabrics for the best effect or all from different scraps of fabric. It is important that the same *type* of fabric should be used throughout. If different kinds of fabric are used, the seams are liable to break open. Using the smaller template, draw and cut out 12 paper shapes. They must be very accurately cut or the patchwork will not lie flat.

Making and joining patches Pin a backing paper to the wrong side of a fabric shape, centring it (diagram 3).

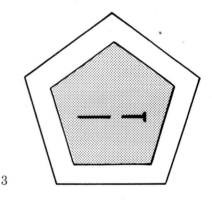

3

Fold the turnings to the wrong side and baste to the backing paper (diagrams 4 and 5). When all the backing papers have been basted to the fabric shapes, place two patches together, right sides facing, and oversew together using tiny stitches

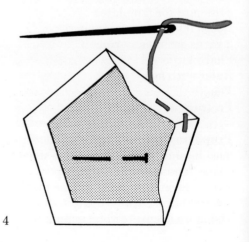

4

(diagram 6). Do not tie a knot at the end of the thread – lay the end along the tops of the patches and oversew over it.

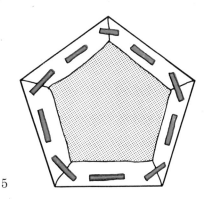

5

Push the needle through the fabric only, at right angles to the edge so that the stitches are neat. To fasten off, work back about four stitches.

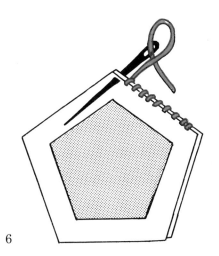

6

Several patches can be joined together continuously but remember to strengthen the corners with two or three stitches. When 11 patches have been joined, remove the backing papers very carefully by cutting the basting stitches and turn the ball to the right side. Stitch the final patch into position along two sides only, keeping the

backing paper in position for the moment.

Finishing the perfume ball Fill the ball with lavender quite tightly and then stitch the remaining three sides of the last patch. Just before the last stitches are made, fold and stitch a cluster of ribbon loops (diagram 7) and push the ends into the ball. Close off the last patch, securing the ribbon ends. Make a 6 inch hanging loop and stitch this into the middle of the small cluster of ribbon loops.

7

Note: Although the foregoing is the technique for patchwork, when flat pieces of work are being done, the finishing off technique is different.

Finishing off flat patchwork When all the patches are joined, press the patches on the wrong side with a warm iron, keeping the backing papers in position. Take out the paper shapes and baste all round the edge of the work to keep the turnings of the edge patches secure. Press again to remove any marks made by the basting. Mount on to lining or on to the main article with slip stitches. Large areas of patchwork will need to be caught down to the lining at regular points.

2 squares = 1 inch

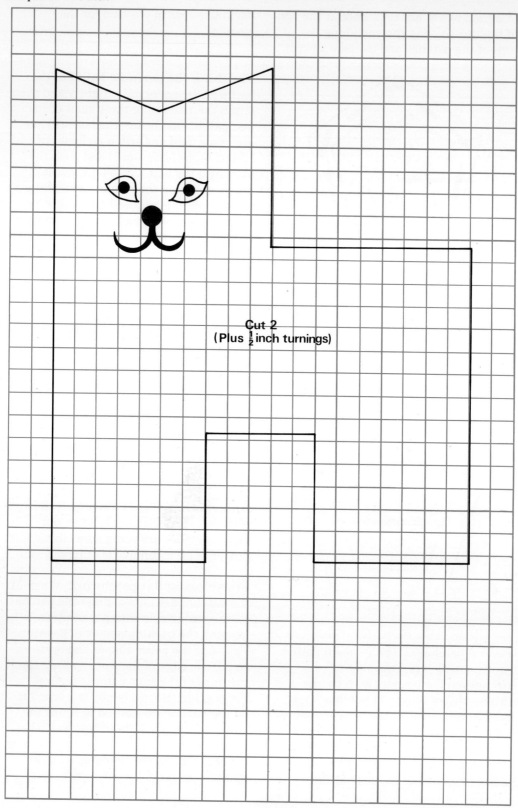

Cut 2
(Plus $\frac{1}{2}$ inch turnings)

*Perfume ball, patchwork cat, patchwork felt
pig*

Patchwork felt pig

illustration on page 11

Felt is much easier to use in patchwork because backing papers do not need to be used.

Materials:
1¼ inch pentagon template
Pink felt
Black felt
Kapok filling
Matching threads

Cut out 12 pentagon shapes in pink felt and two in black for the ears. Stitch 11 together into a ball. Turn the pig right side out and then stitch the last patch in so that the seams of this patch show on the right side. This patch is the pig's snout. Stuff the pig with kapok quite tightly and close the last patch. Cut four circles of pink felt ½ inch diameter. Embroider two black nostrils on the top one. Glue the circles one on top of the other. Glue to the pig's snout. Gather one edge of the two black ear pieces and stitch to the top of the pig's head. Cut four strips of black felt, 3 inches long by ½ inch wide and roll them up to make feet. Secure with stitches and then glue and finally stitch the feet to the underside of the body. Cut a thin 2 inch strip of black felt for the tail. Draw it up on a piece of black cotton to curl it and stitch in place.

To make other patchwork animals, try green felt for a frog and add two long arms and legs. Make an owl using light and dark brown felt or a cat using black and white. A rabbit or a panda could also be made on the pentagon ball shape.

Felt balls can be made using the same basic instructions. Cut the pentagon shape with 2½ inch sides and cut 12 shapes from felt using bright, primary colours. Push a bell into the middle of the ball as you are stuffing it.

Patchwork cat

illustrated on page 11

This charming patchwork cat is very easy to make and uses a quick random patchwork technique.

It is made from square and rectangular pieces of fabric, cut out with pinking shears and joined, overlapping, with machine zigzag stitch. If a swing needle machine is not available, overlap the patches ¼ inch, baste together and join with straight machine stitching, worked on the right side.

Materials
Scraps of cotton fabric
Kapok filling
Scraps of blue and black felt
Anchor stranded embroidery thread, crimson

Make up two pieces of patchwork 11 inches wide by 12 inches deep using method already described under 'Perfume ball'. Draw out and cut a paper pattern from the graph pattern given on page 10. Cut out two cat shapes using the paper pattern. On one piece embroider the mouth in stem stitch. Cut out the eyes, pupils and nose from felt. Glue them in position. Stab stitch to secure. Add sequins. Make up a strip of patchwork pieces 3¼ inches wide by 47 inches long. Using ½ inch seams, join the strip to one cat piece, matching raw edges and right sides facing. Join the second side of the cat to the strip, leaving a gap of 4 inches under the body for inserting the filling. Stuff the cat and close the opening with neat oversewing.

Papier mâché

Papier mâché is a most fascinating craft and can be an inexpensive way of making gifts. The amusing savings pig, the tumbler dolls, the Easter egg and the comfit bowl were made using a layering technique.

Materials
Newspaper
Tissue paper
Paste
Gesso glue
Paints

Making the paste Some papier mâché enthusiasts use diluted white glue or wallpaper paste but a simple flour and water paste works just as well. Mix a small quantity of plain white flour to a thick paste with cold water. Add common salt to the mixture (about 1 tablespoon to $\frac{1}{2}$ lb. flour). This preserves the paste for several days while you are working on the project. Keep the paste in the refrigerator or a cool place. Pour boiling water on to the paste, stirring all the time. The paste will thicken again and become translucent. Dilute to the consistency of thick cream.

Preparing the paper Newspaper is best for papier mâché – magazine pages are usually too thick to absorb the paste. Tear up a quantity of newspaper first into strips and then into pieces about 1 inch square.

The technique In the layering technique, the newspaper is first dipped into the paste, the excess removed with the fingers of the other hand and then applied in layers to the surface of a prepared mould. The mould is coated with an oil (such as cooking oil) so that the papier mâché shape can be removed easily when it has dried out.
Various objects can be used as moulds. For round shapes, balloons, inverted bowls, cups and some kinds of fruit can be used. The savings pig, for instance, was made on an inflated balloon. The fall-over dolls were made on blown eggs and the Easter egg was made on an orange. A melon is also a good shape for making a savings pig and cups make good moulds for papier mâché puppet heads. Pretty bowls, plates, dishes and trays can be made using the layering technique if a similar utensil is used for the mould. After oiling the mould carefully build the layers of papier mâché up on the *underside* or outside of the utensil.

Decorating papier mâché Papier mâché can be decorated with poster colours and then varnished afterwards, with modeller's enamel paints, with layers of coloured tissue added after the shape has dried or with various shapes cut out of cardboard. String, dipped in gesso, can be glued in curlicue designs on to the sides of bowls or on trays and painted in a contrasting colour when the gesso has completely dried. Sequins, beads and shells, glued to the surface of papier mâché are a quick and attractive form of decoration.

Savings pig

illustrated on page 15

Materials
Newspaper
Flour and water paste
A balloon
1 inch curtain ring
Tissue paper
Gesso powder or paste
Enamel paints or poster paints
Transfers if desired
Scraps of felt for ears
All purpose adhesive
2 large bowls
1 pudding basin
Sharp knife

Inflate the balloon to about the size of a child's head. Knot the opening. Cover the balloon's surface with oil and then rest it on a bowl or basin so that about half of the balloon is above the bowl's rim (diagram 1). Tear up the newspaper

1

into 1 inch squares. Dip pieces of torn newspaper into the prepared paste and cover the entire surface of the balloon with layers of paper. When two complete layers have been applied, leave to dry overnight. Apply two more layers of newspaper then make the pig's snout as follows:

14

Stand the balloon on end in the basin, tied end down. Tear a long strip of newspaper about 1 inch wide, dip it into the paste and roll it up, adding more strips until you have a circular lump of papier mâché about 2 inches across. Place this in position on the balloon mould and paste small pieces of paper up the sides until it is firmly held. Smooth the snout underneath so that it blends into the pig's body (diagram 2). Cut open a curtain ring and push the cut ends into the snout. Leave to dry overnight. Work one more layer of paper all over the mould.

2

To make the feet, tear long strips of newspaper about 1 inch wide. Paste and then roll them up until you have stumps about $\frac{3}{4}$ inch in diameter. Balance each foot in position on the underside of the pig's body and paste small pieces of paper up the sides until the feet are held firmly as for the snout. Leave to dry and then add three more layers of paper all over the pig. When the papier mâché is completely dry, stick a needle into the balloon through the knot and deflate it. Draw the balloon out through the hole carefully. Make a tail from a piece of tissue paper twisted and pasted. Leave it until dry and then insert the tail into the hole. Glue in position and secure with pasted paper pieces. Cut a hole in

Savings pig, tumbler dolls, Easter egg, comfit bowl

the pig's back using a sharp pointed knife, to put the coins in. Sandpaper over to smooth out any obvious lumps but if you have applied the newspaper evenly there should not be any. Paint mixed gesso all over the pig and leave to dry. Apply one layer of white tissue paper all over the gesso – this makes a good painting surface. Paint the pig with modeller's enamel paints or with poster paints. If poster paints are used, two coats of quick-drying varnish must be applied after the paint is dry. Designs can be painted or, for a quick yet professional-looking decoration, use transfers. Paint in black spots for eyes. Cut two floppy ears (diagram 3) from felt and glue them to the pig's head.

Trace same size

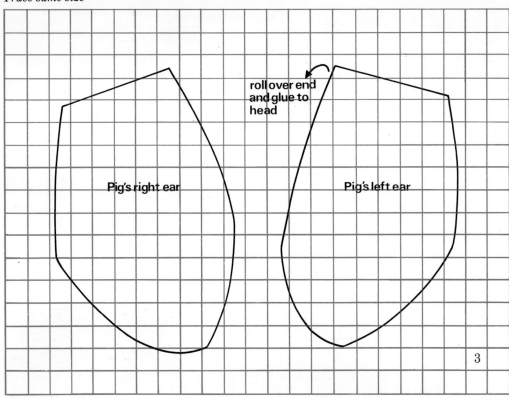

roll over end and glue to head

Pig's right ear

Pig's left ear

3

Tumbler dolls

illustrated on page 15

Tumbler dolls such as these are familiar in many mid-European countries and are usually made of wood. When they are knocked over, they spring upright again. These are made from egg-shells and papier mâché.

Materials
Three raw eggs
White tissue paper
Flour and water paste
Gesso powder or ready-mixed gesso paste
Modeller's enamel paints or poster colours
Lead shot

To prepare the eggs First, blow the eggs. This is done by making a small hole in the shell at both ends. Make a hole first with a thin sharp needle and then enlarge the holes with a thicker needle. Poke into one hole with a long needle to break up the yolk inside. Hold the egg between the thumb and forefinger and, bending over a ready saucer, blow firmly into one of the holes. At first, nothing seems to happen and then a single spot of egg yolk will drop out of the other hole. Persevere and the drops of egg will fall out quite quickly. As the egg empties, hold the egg more carefully and blow more gently or it will smash in your fingers. When all the egg seems to be out, wash the eggshell and leave to dry. You do not need to oil the shell in preparation for papier mâché because the shell mould remains inside the tumbler doll.

Making the tumbler doll Close the hole at the 'blunt' end of the egg with a piece of pasted paper. Enlarge the hole at the pointed end of the egg and drop in some all-purpose adhesive. Drop in three pieces of lead shot and leave the glue to set so that the lead shot is firmly held. Close this hole also with a small piece of tissue paper. Tear up tiny pieces of tissue paper, each about $\frac{1}{2}$ inch square and apply them to the surface of the egg with paste. Build up four or five layers and leave each layer to dry out before applying the next.

When the last layer is dry, apply a thin coat of mixed gesso and then decorate the eggs with paints. For an alternative design, paint the eggs to look like circus clowns.

Easter egg

illustrated on page 15

Oil a large sized orange all over and balance it on a large mug or cup. Apply eight layers of newspaper papier mâché and leave until quite dry. Using a sharp knife, cut lengthwise through the papier mâché and remove the whole orange. Cover the inside and the outside of the two halves with two layers of tissue paper pieces and if the surface is still not smooth enough, paint with mixed gesso. Decorate the egg with enamel paint or poster colours, afterwards finishing with two layers of quick drying varnish.

Place a gift inside the egg and tie the two halves together with ribbon.

Comfit bowl

illustrated on page 15

The comfit bowl is made on an upturned glass bowl, oiled with cooking oil. Apply newspaper papier mâché until eight layers have been built up and then two layers of white tissue paper for a smooth finish. Paint the bowl with modeller's enamels. It is better not to use poster colours for papier mâché dishes and trays.

For an interesting surface decoration on bowls such as this, cut out shapes in thin card and glue them to the surface of the bowl. Give the entire bowl two layers of thickly mixed gesso and sand down until smooth. Paint the shapes, which are slightly in relief from the surface, with contrast colours.

Papier mâché bowls and trays cannot be put into water but they can be cleaned with a damp cloth.

Decoupage

Decoupage is a centuries old craft, now enjoying a revival in popularity. The technique involves cutting out prints, pasting them on to suitable furniture or furnishings and varnishing the piece. Even if you cannot draw at all, you can create beautiful or amusing pieces of decoupage which will make wonderful gifts. It is possible to utilize furniture which has been cast aside, such as old sewing boxes, occasional tables, book racks or trays and with a little imagination, transform them into pieces which look every bit as good as those decorated items seen in exclusive decorator's shops. Alternatively, decoupage can be used to produce gay and modern accessories.

The cheese board illustrated was decorated with cut-outs from a sheet of gift wrapping.
The egg cups are made of wood, painted with white emulsion paint and then decorated with tiny cut-out flower sprays from a magazine advertisement.

Materials
Scissors Cutting out must be done very carefully and cuticle scissors are the best for the job. These have a curved blade and are about 3 inches long overall. Buy the very best you can afford – it is a worthwhile investment if you want to enjoy doing decoupage.

Paste Only a water soluble paste is suitable for decoupage. There are several available and they are usually white or translucent. Many **glues** are not water soluble and should not be used.

Varnish Professionals use good quality lacquers for the craft, leaving the surface to dry out for a whole day. Modern polyurethane varnishes dry in about half the time and produce a good hard finish. For decoupage, gloss varnish is better than matt as gloss enables the print to show through better. Spray varnishes can be used for the first two or three coats if you hesitate to use the liquid kind immediately, but they are not suitable for the whole job as the applied coat is so thin. It would need more than 100 coats to get the right finished effect.

Brushes Varnishing brushes must be the very best that can be obtained. The width of the brush, of course, depends on the size of the piece you are working on, but try to have one which requires the least number of strokes to cover the surface of the piece. Choose a brush with a soft bristle and if you insist on the best quality available, the bristles are less likely to fall out and fasten themselves into your decoupage. Nothing is more irritating than having to pick up a fine brush bristle which has fastened itself right in the middle of a beautiful piece of decoupage, and you can easily damage the surface trying to pick up the bristle.

Other equipment A bowl of warm water and a small sponge; baby buds or cottonwool on a toothpick; white blotting paper for removing excess water; solvent in a jar for the varnishing brush; a sharp blade; lintless cloth or old nylon tights; fine sandpaper; fine steel wool; wax polish.

Preparing the surface First, the

18

Decoupage cheese board, egg cups

surface of the item to be decorated must be absolutely smooth. Fill any dents with plastic wood or wood putty and when the filler has hardened, sand the entire surface, finishing off by rubbing down with steel wool. When the surface is quite smooth, paint or stain it. If you are working on natural wood and you like the colour, leave it as it is. If you are painting, water paints, oil paints or enamel can be used. Before painting, seal the surface with a commercial sealer, selected for the type of paint you are using. When the paint or stain is dry, rub down again with steel wool and dust off with a lintless cloth – old nylon stockings or tights are ideal.

Prints Ideally, the prints used should be on thin paper, otherwise they are difficult to cut out and it takes many more layers of varnish to cover them. Studios which specialize in decoupage produce books of delightful designs by such artists as Jean Pillement, Watteau and Boucher. These are printed on a suitable paper for the craft but if they are not easily available there are wonderful designs to be had from other sources. Gift wrapping papers are often well designed and can provide a good source of material. Greetings cards are sometimes suitable or illustrations from magazines and seed catalogues could be used. Search out old wallpaper sample books, visit your local crafts shop and look at their stock of prints and transfers, and most exciting of all, try old books – sometimes the engraved chapter headings and frontispiece pages can provide charming designs. Black and white prints can be hand-coloured and Derwent oil pencils are best for this. However, if you prefer to use black and white prints just as they are, they can look superb on a white painted background.
If you are planning to decorate an old item, first remove all the original finish.

Metal objects can be decoupaged, but every spot of rust must be removed and a rust inhibitor applied before painting. Any colour of paint can be used under decoupage but if white is used, note that it will turn ivory under the coats of varnish.

Cutting out To learn to cut out really well requires practice but you will find it is a most relaxing occupation. A good way to get the feel of cutting paper is to practise on cutting scallops. Hold the paper in your left hand (or right hand if you are left handed). Hold the scissors with the curved tips pointing away from you, third finger and thumb in the scissors. Rest the scissors on the index finger. The hand holding the scissors does not move, it merely opens and closes the blades. The paper is fed into the blades by moving the left hand. To practise cutting scallops, turn the hand holding the paper towards the right and at the same time, slowly close the scissor blades on the paper. Cutting out in this way gives the cut edge a 'feathered' look and makes pasting down far easier. Before actually cutting out a print, spray it first with a fixative, obtained from art shops. This gives the paper more body, helps to prevent it breaking up during pasting and also helps to preserve the colours from the varnish.
There are no absolute rules about cutting out; it is advisable to avoid long straight cuts – the paper should be moved gently during cutting to obtain a slightly serrated edge and inside corners should be crisp rather than rounded. But whether you prefer to cut round the outline first or whether you feel you would like to cut the inside portions of the design first is up to you.

Pasting down If you are pasting down small pieces of cut-out, it is easier to apply the adhesive to the back of the paper with a small brush. Spread the adhesive right to the edge of the piece or the edges will curl or bubbles will appear under the print. Place the print on the prepared surface and press it down, exerting pressure from the centre out towards the edges. Some excess adhesive may be forced out. Remove this carefully with a small sponge dipped in warm water and squeezed out. If you are pasting down larger pieces you may find it easier to spread adhesive on the surface of the object, then press the print down on to the adhesive. To remove excess adhesive from the small inside areas of the background use a baby bud stick or twist a piece of cotton wool round a toothpick. When all the cut-outs have been pasted down, check to see that all the edges are quite flat and that there are no air bubbles. Air bubbles can be dealt with if they do occur by carefully slitting the paper with a sharp blade and inserting more adhesive with a toothpick. Leave the pasted prints to dry out very thoroughly.

Varnishing The final stage of decoupage can seem the most tedious of all but the care with which you varnish and rub down can make all the difference in the world to your finished piece. First of all, spray the entire surface with fixative and rub the surface down with a lintless cloth. Apply the varnish with long smooth strokes and work on a flat surface. Leave the varnish to dry completely before applying the next coat. A finished piece can have as many as 30 coats of varnish. It is necessary to apply as many coats as this to give it the perfect finish which is typical of good decoupage. Sometimes, if

the prints are on very thin paper you can get away with as few as sixteen to twenty coats of varnish – but it very much depends on the use for which the item is intended. Trinket boxes, which are likely to be handled for instance, would be better with the full 30 coats. For a decorative kitchen wall plaque, a fewer number of coats might be sufficient.

In most homes, there is inevitably some dust in the air and if you can make a kind of tent from a large plastic bag or a sheet of Cellophane, this will provide some cover while the varnish is drying out.

After 10 coats have been applied or when you can no longer feel the edge of the paper cut-out with a finger tip, sanding down begins. Wrap a small piece of fine sandpaper round a matchbox and rub the surface all over in a circular motion. Dust the surface off, wash it clean with a dampened sponge and leave to dry. Now rub the surface again with the fine steel wool and wipe the surface clean. You are now ready for the next coat of varnish. Continue giving coats of varnish, rubbing down between coats, until the entire surface is quite flat and the prints are showing through with a dull, soft glow.

Give a final polish with good wax polish.

Some ideas for decoupage gifts: boxes of all kinds for trinkets, cigarettes, playing cards, stamps or handkerchiefs; tea trays and cocktail trays; small tables, wastebaskets, door finger panels, wall plaques, wooden household utensils, wooden or metal jewellery, shoe and belt buckles, paperweights.

Beltmaking

Belts make marvellous gifts and can be made from all kinds of materials. Ribbons and braids, for instance, mounted on belt stiffening, make colourful, gaily patterned belts; felt, trimmed with narrow braid and finished with eyelet fastenings, makes a charming peasant belt.

A sporty-looking link belt can be made from scraps of suede or leather and, of course, a belt worked in quick-stitch on canvas has a special cachet all of its own. Belts take comparatively little time to make and junk shops, you will find, are a treasure house for unusual buckles and clasps.

Ribbon and braid belts

illustrated opposite

It is advisable to choose the buckle first and to have it with you when you are choosing the ribbon or braid. Not only will you be able to make sure that you havĕ chosen the best ribbon to enhance the buckle but you will also be able to check that the width of the ribbon fits the buckle bar.

Ribbons and braids are available up to quite wide widths. A 3 inch wide woven ribbon will make a superb belt used just as it is but do consider the narrower kinds. Sometimes, a ribbon or braid with a geometric design takes on a new and exciting look if two or more narrow strips are mounted side by side.

The red and white ribbon belt illustrated is made up of three widths of diagonally striped ½ inch wide ribbon with the middle strip reversed to make a chevron design.

If a single length of ribbon or braid is being used, buy a length to the waist measurements plus 6 inches. If narrower widths are being used mounted together to make a wide belt, multiply the waist-plus-six measurement by the number of lengths you are planning to use.

Materials
Embroidered ribbons or braids
Belt stiffening or other stiff interlacing
Backing material such as taffeta or silk
Fabric adhesive
Suitable buckle
Strong all-purpose adhesive

Cut a piece of belt stiffening or interfacing to the exact width of the ribbon and to the waist measurement plus 6 inches. Cut one end of the stiffening into a point (diagram 1) and then trim the two cut edges (A and B) back a further ¼ inch. Trim the other short end of the stiffening (C) ¼ inch.

Ribbon and braid belts, felt peasant belt

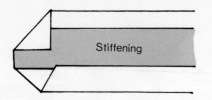

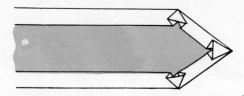

Stiffening

Cut a piece of lining fabric to the width and length of the belt, (waist-plus-six), plus 1¼ inches on both measurements. Place the stiffening down on the wrong side of the lining fabric and fold over the ⅝th inch turnings all round. Mitre the corners neatly and fold the lining over the pointed end of the belt as shown (see diagram 2). Glue the turnings down onto the stiffening using fabric adhesive but use very little or the adhesive may seep through and spoil the look of the inside of the belt. Place a weight on the pointed end and leave the belt to dry.

While the belt is drying, cut a point on the right hand end of the ribbon, clip into the point ¼ inch and turn under ¼ inch turnings. Turn the other short end of the ribbon under ¼ inch and press. To mount the ribbon, spread adhesive on the belt itself, not on the ribbon, taking the adhesive to within ⅛th inch of the edges. This is so that any excess adhesive can spread a little without spoiling the ribbon or the lining. Use the minimum amount of adhesive and spread it as evenly as possible.

Place the ribbon down onto the glued surface of the stiffening and press it firmly into position with the flat of the hand. Leave the belt to dry. When quite dry, slip the buckle onto the square end – this is the left hand side of the belt so make sure that the buckle is the right way up if it has that kind of shape – and fold the end of the belt under over the buckle bar for about 2 inches. Glue the belt over the buckle bar using all-purpose adhesive and leave to dry under a weight. Secure with oversewing stitches.

Felt peasant belt

illustrated on page 23

Materials

Strip of felt to the waist measurement less 2 inches and 3½ inches wide.
Narrow braid or ribbon, twice the length of the belt plus 9 inches.
Six eyelets
1 yard contrasting coloured silk cord

Place the strip of felt on a flat surface and fold in the short ends 1 inch on the top side of the fabric. Glue these ends down. Cut two pieces of the trim, 3½ inches wide and mount these along the cut edges of the folded ends.

Cut the remaining trim into two equal lengths and glue along both long sides of the belt and over the short end strips. Turn ½ inch under at both ends to neaten.

Make three equidistant marks on both edges of the belt fronts, ¼ inch in from the edge and insert eyelets.

Lace the belt together with the cord. If eyelets cannot be obtained, finish off the holes with closely worked buttonhole stitch, using a brightly contrasting thread.

Norweave belt

illustrated on page 27

Norweave embroidery, which as its name suggests came from Norway, is especially recommended for beginners in canvas work, or for those in a hurry, as

3 by 28 inches lining material
Matching thread for lining
3 press studs

Note The length of the belt can be adjusted by approx 1¾ inches which is the measurement of one pattern repeat (18 stitches).

Point shaping

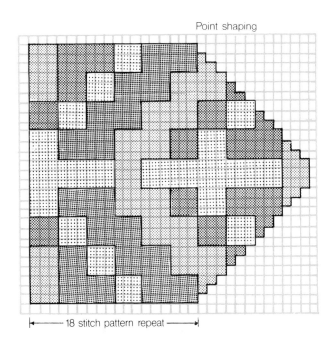

|←——— 18 stitch pattern repeat ———→|

you get fairly quick results. It consists of blocks of satin stitch worked over three horizontal and vertical double threads of canvas. It can be used for pictures, panels, cushions or anywhere where a bold design is suitable.

Materials
3½ by 28 inches of double thread canvas, 10 threads to the inch
2 skeins each Anchor Tapisserie Wool in dark, medium and light colours

Start working the design from the chart leaving 4 double threads unworked at each edge for turning in when making up. The satin stitch here is worked over three double threads each way. Try not to catch your wool on the raw edges of the canvas or it will fray and weaken.

To make up Press the completed embroidery lightly, with damp cloth and warm iron. Fold over turnings to wrong side of work and baste, neatening the point. Baste hems on lining to correspond and handstitch lining in position on wrong side of embroidery.

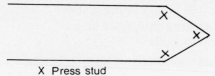

X Press stud

Sew press studs as indicated on diagram, making sure that the pattern matches when belt is fastened.

Suede belts

illustrated on page 27

Smart suede and leather belts can be very simply made by cutting a strip of the material to the waist measurement plus six inches and fastening it to a beautiful buckle.

Norweave belt, suede belt

Decorating china and pottery

Old crafts are being revived and decorating china and pottery is one of the newest 'revivals'.

China painting

There are two ways of approaching painting china and pottery. The way you choose depends on whether or not the piece is going to be subjected to hard wear and constant washing up.

China subjected to hard wear

If the pieces are going to be used every day and washed up, such as cups and saucers, mugs and plates, the decoration must be more or less permanent and stand up to being immersed in detergent. For this kind of decoration a special cool-bake enamel is used, obtainable from craft shops. The enamel is simply painted on to the surface of the piece and each colour left to dry before the next is applied. When all the colours of the design are completed, the piece is placed in a cold oven which is set for 350°F, gas mark 4. When the oven reaches this temperature, turn off and leave to cool down. Under no circumstances should the oven be opened during the process. Open only when it has cooled completely. The piece of china should now be permanently decorated. However, it is wiser not to clean decorated china with steel wool or the design might be damaged!

China used as decoration

Pottery or china which is not intended for hard wear, such as flower pots, kitchen crocks, ornaments etc., can be decorated with modeller's enamels or with Polymer water colours. Once again, colours should be applied and left to dry thoroughly before the next colour is applied. Use any kind of brush which seems right for the job, – soft sable brushes, sizes 2 and 3 are ideal.

Stencilling pottery

Stencilling is great fun to do and, if you cannot draw, designs can be taken from books, posters, gift wrapping papers or greetings cards. You might look at the pottery section of your local museum too and study the traditional folk designs, adapting them to your pieces.
Choose designs which are simple in outline and avoid those with fine lines or sharp points. Inevitably a little paint floods under the stencil and while the effect can be quite attractive on a simple design, it can spoil a complicated one.

Materials

Pot or jar with unindented surface
Fast drying spray enamel
Stencil paper (available from art and craft shops)
Sharp crafts knife
Tracing paper
Rubber cement
Masking tape (available from art shops)
Newspaper

Trace off your selected design and glue

the tracing down on to the stencil paper with rubber cement. Cut out the stencil with the sharp point of the knife and tape the stencil to the china with masking tape. Mask the areas not to be

spray down on to it and, studying the manufacturer's instructions first, hold the spray can about 12 inches away from the piece. Spray in short bursts and avoid applying too much paint as it will

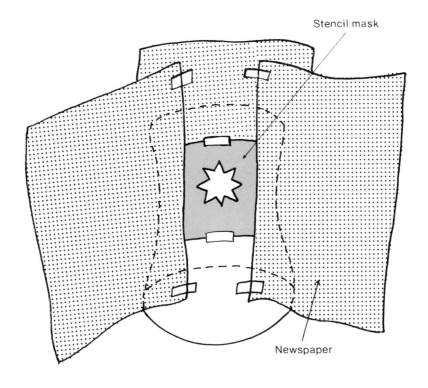

Stencil mask

Newspaper

stencilled with newspaper, taping it down firmly (see diagram).
Place the piece on the floor on several sheets of newspaper so that you can

bleed under the stencil edges.
Very messy edges can be cleaned up by scratching away after the paint is dry, using a sharp razor blade.

Collage

Collage is great fun to do because there are so few rules to follow. It is simply a technique of sticking different kinds of materials down on to a background. Basically, there are three types of collage: paper collage, which uses different kinds of paper; fabric collage where mostly fabrics are used, with perhaps some beads, sequins or buttons for additional texture, and lastly, three-dimensional collage where all kinds of materials can be utilized – nails, straw, raffia, string, pieces of glass, pasta, seeds, safety pins – practically anything which looks decorative and can be glued down. The collage picture 'Fish dinner' uses fabrics and buttons. You may want to try the fish picture for yourself and a diagram is given on page 33 from which you can make a paper pattern of the various pieces. However collage is such a personal craft that you will probably want to try something original yourself. Look for inspiration in magazines, books, posters or on gift wrappings or greetings cards or work freehand. Flower studies are delightful subjects for fabric collage and so are still lifes of fruit and objects. You might even try a portrait – it could be fun!

Essential equipment

A few tools are needed for collage: soft pencils, a ruler, some tracing paper, cardboard, large and small scissors, pins, a sharp craft knife and, of course, adhesives. Three kinds of adhesive are used, but you will need only two of them for the fish picture. For heavy fabrics and for adding trims, a fabric adhesive such as Copydex is used. For light fabrics and for paper, an adhesive such as Polycell is ideal and for three

dimensional objects, such as buttons, a clear all-purpose adhesive is used. You will need either Copydex or Polycell and a clear all-purpose adhesive.

Fabrics

Keep scraps of fabric in a separate bag just for collage pictures. It does not matter how small the piece, it will probably prove perfect somewhere in a design. It is not worthwhile buying remnants for collage but you may find that you can pick up interesting fabrics at junk sales or white elephant sales. Old garments, washed and with the good pieces cut away, can provide the collage enthusiast with some valuable colours and textures.

Firmly woven fabrics often make the best backgrounds but one cannot generalise about this. Loosely woven fabrics, such as tweeds, can give marvellous textural effects and, if such a material is being considered, it may be better to mount it on a non-woven interfacing first. Cut background fabrics at least 2 inches larger all round for turnings.

Loosely woven fabrics to be used in the design are best mounted on non-woven interfacing before cutting them out: other fabrics can either be cut out with a clean edge before mounting on the background, can be frayed or have the edges turned under. It depends on the fabric and the effect you are trying to achieve.

Method

Make a rough drawing of your picture on tracing paper first. When you are satisfied with the design, which should be kept to the simplest possible shapes,

Hand-decorated china

make another tracing which you can cut up for patterns. It is possible to cut into fabrics freehand, but beginners often find it easier to cut from paper patterns. If you decide to draw out your shape directly onto the back of the fabric before cutting out, remember that the design must be reversed or you will find that your shape is the wrong way round when you come to mount it. Place the background fabric flat on a table and arrange the various components of the design upon it. When you are satisfied that the colours and textures look right, start by glueing down the parts of the design which are in the background first, mounting the foreground units over them. Do not stick anything down until you are quite satisfied that an edge may not need to be tucked behind another piece for the best effect.

Mounting collage pictures

Small collage pictures, such as 'Fish dinner,' see page 34, can be mounted on cardboard. Cut the cardboard to the finished picture size. Spread all-purpose adhesive on the edges of the card on the wrong side. Spread adhesive about 2 inches from the edges. Place the fabric picture down on a flat surface, right side down. Place the prepared card on the wrong side of the fabric, with the prepared side uppermost. Fold the turnings over onto the glue, mitreing the corners neatly (diagram 1).

Glue the corners and leave to dry. For framing, mount the finished collage on another piece of good quality cardboard so that a neat border shows round the picture. 'Fish dinner' was simply mounted on card and two curtain rings were attached to the corners with small pieces of ribbon (diagram 2, page 34).

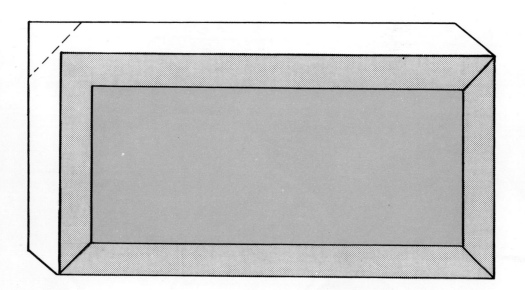

1

2 squares = 1 inch

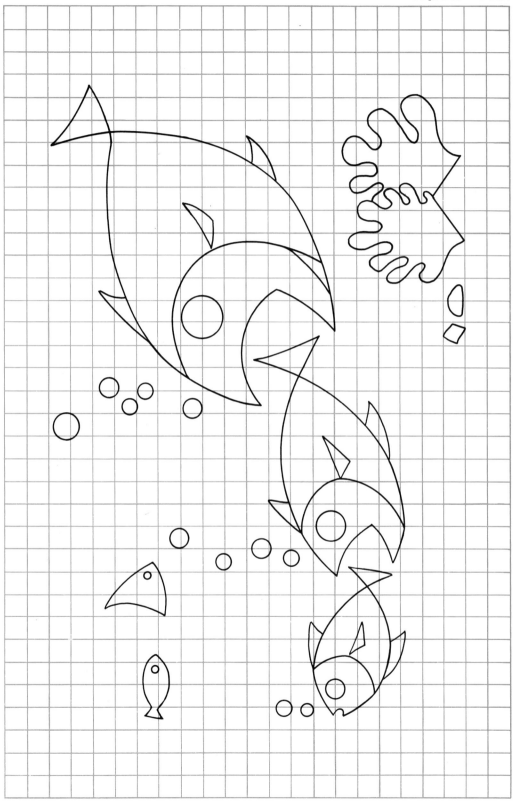

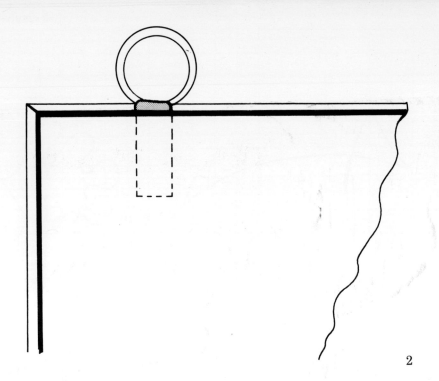

2

Fish dinner

The background fabric of the collage is a piece of blue poplin. On this, scraps of green and blue patterned organza are mounted for the sea effect. The small fish in the background are cut out of grey green velvet with sequin eyes and these, together with the darker clump of seaweed are mounted next. Pale blue nylon net goes next over the entire picture. The fish bodies are cut from a patterned cotton fabric which was chosen because it has a scaly effect and, in fact, this fabric inspired the whole picture. The fish heads are cut from velvet and the eyes are buttons of different sizes. The fish bubbles are small circles of interfacing material, chosen because it has a slightly transparent look.

Fish dinner collage

Tie-dye and Fabric painting

Tie-dyeing is an ancient craft, practised almost all over the world at different times. Modern cold-water dyes and fixes make tie-dyeing comparatively simple to do and a wide variety of gifts can be made from everyday, natural fabrics. Cushion covers, towels, tea cloths, bed linen, neckties, scarves, lampshades are all possible tie-dye projects.

Materials

Very little basic equipment is needed for tie-dye. The most important is a large utensil to use as a dye bath. Using cold water dyes, this can be made of metal, plastic, pottery or glass. Other equipment, depending on the tie you are using, might include string, pieces of stone, corks and rubber bands, and clothes pegs.

Basic technique

This consists of taking a piece of fabric and tying, folding, binding, knotting or sewing it so that when the fabric is dipped in the prepared dyebath, the colour penetrates only the untied areas of the cloth. Patterns appear on those areas which have been partially protected from the dye and complex patterns can be achieved by tying an area, then untying and retying and dyeing again in a different colour. Cold water dyes, which are intended for natural fabrics, produce a fast colour and the tie-dye pattern will therefore last. Man-made fibre fabrics use a special dye and this is not as fast. Fabrics which have special finishes should not be used as they resist dyes. Wool fabrics should be avoided as the garment's shape can be spoiled.

36

Quantities of dye As a rough guide, one small tin of cold water dye will dye approximately 6 ozs of dry fabric. A dress weighs about 1 lb. so if you were planning to dye this amount of fabric (about 2–3 yards) in two colours, you would need two tins of *each* colour.

Preparing the dye bath It is important to use a large enough dye bath – this is the secret of satisfactory dyeing. Make up the dye according to the manufacturer's instructions and add, as instructed, 1 sachet of cold water dye fix and four tablespoons of common salt for each tin of dye used.

Preparing the fabric If a soft effect is required, use the fabric dry; if the pattern is to be crisp, wet the fabric first. Tie the fabric in any of the ways illustrated on pages 37–45. Immerse the knotted fabric in the bath, leaving it for the recommended period of time. If a piece is to be dyed in two or more colours, the part which is not to be dyed can be protected by tying it up in a polythene bag.

'His' and 'Hers' guest towels

illustrated on 39

Materials

Two cotton towelling squares
2 polythene bags
1 tin each of Dylon Cold Water dyes in Coral and French blue
2 sachets of cold dye fix.
8 tablespoons common salt

(continued on page 42)

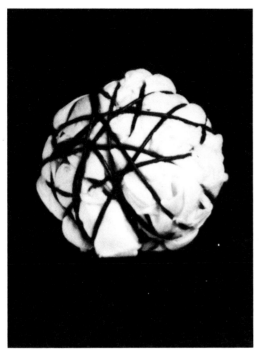 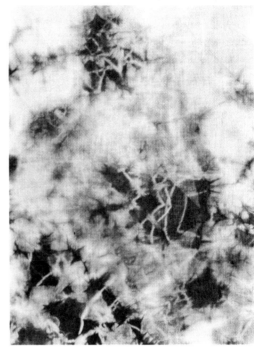

Marbling: Cloth screwed up into a ball and bound tightly.

Dyeing sample *wet* gives crisper resist.   Dyeing sample *dry* gives softer resist.

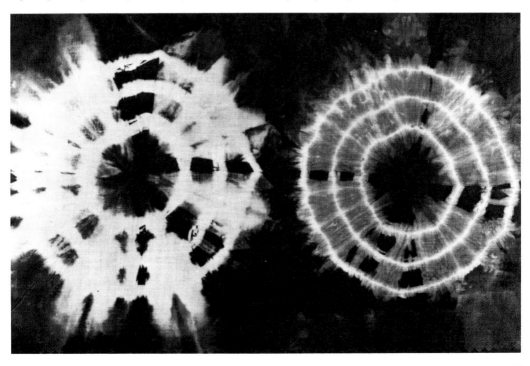

 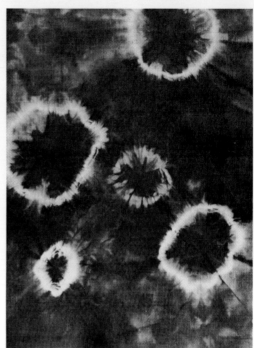

Clump: Small and large tufts picked up and bound.

Tritik (Stitching): Double rows of stitching are pulled up very tight and knotted off securely.

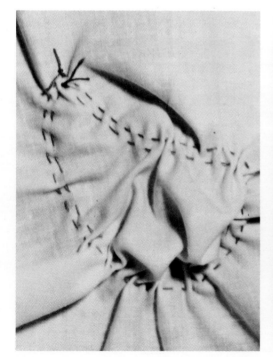 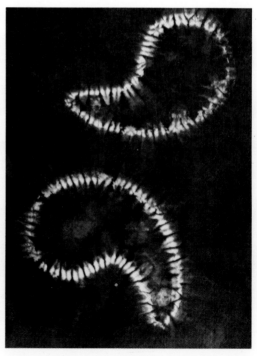

'His' and 'Hers' guest towels

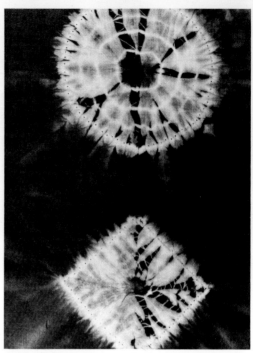

Safety-pin: Oval and Diamond picked up with safety-pin then bound. Oval with line binding, diamond with open binding.

Ruching: Cloth rolled round cord or doubled string and ruched.

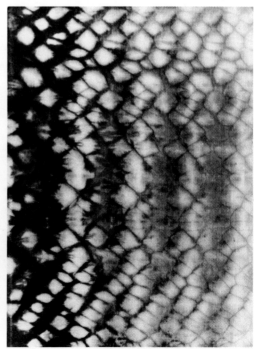

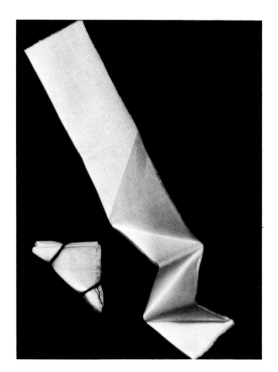 

Triangle: Cloth folded into four lengthwise, then folded back into a right angled triangle and bound securely.

Knotting: Length with three knots.

Draw the lettering on the towels with a soft pencil, copying the photograph. Using strong thread, knotted securely at one end, run small basting stitches over the pencilled lines. Leave a long length of thread. Damp the towelling and pull up the thread really tightly, binding the end of the thread round the bunched fabric. Put half the towel into the polythene bag (up to the diagonal line) and secure it very firmly by tying with

up to one hour, stirring occasionally. Rinse off excess dye. Remove the polythene bag, remove the stitches and wash the towel in hot suds, rinsing until the water runs clear.

Fabric painted gifts

illustrated opposite

Fabric paints using cold water dyes are comparatively new but they are

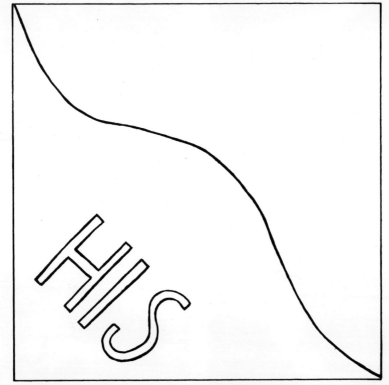

Guest towel, showing lettering position and diagonal line

string, to prevent the dye seeping in. Make up the French blue dye. Immerse the exposed area of the towel in the dye and leave for up to one hour, stirring occasionally. Remove from the dye-bath and rinse off excess dye. Put the dyed half of the towel into a polythene bag and seal tightly. Steep the other half of the towel in Coral dye for

fascinating to use and very easy. Really lovely gifts can be made from odds and ends of fabric and a few tins of dye. An old bed sheet could be made to produce dozens of delightful soft toys or some animal day-bed cushions. Simple garments can be personalized with names or mottoes and make very acceptable gifts.

42

Fabric painted gifts

Materials

For each colour,
   1 tin of Dylon cold water dye
   1 packet of Paintex and cold dye fix
   (these are sold together)
Hot water
Fabric, either white or coloured
Paint brushes
Polythene sheeting

Most natural fabrics, cotton, silk and
linen, take fabric painting very well. It
is worth noting that after dye-painting,
neither bleaches nor biological
detergents should be used in washing.
Dye-painted items will, however, stand
up to boiling.
Wash and iron the fabric. Lay it on a
piece of polythene sheeting and draw
in the design with a soft pencil. If a
ready-made garment is being painted,
slip a piece of polythene sheeting inside
the garment so that the colour does not
seep through to the back. Mix the dye-
paints according to the manufacturer's
instructions. Paint in the design and
leave to dry for up to six hours. The
longer the paint is left on the fabric, the
deeper the colour will be. When the
fabric and paint is quite dry, wash off
the excess dye in cold water, then wash
in hot suds and rinse until the water is
clear. The painted design is now
absolutely permanent.

Soft toys

illustrated on page 43

All the toys illustrated were made from
an old bed sheet. The lion, dog and
kangaroo were made using a commercial
paper pattern. The sheep was traced
from a child's picture book and $\frac{1}{4}$ inch
turnings were allowed all round for
seams.
The frog was also made from sheeting.
The fabric for the frog was dyed
Nasturtium. Coloured fabrics could, of
course, be used if you prefer.

To make the toys Cut out the pattern
pieces from the sheeting and lay them on
polythene. Draw out the designs in soft
pencil and paint them in. Finish the dye
process and the laundering process as
instructed. Sew up the pattern pieces and
stuff the toys with sponge chips or with
cut-up nylon tights. This ensures that
the toys are washable.
Cold water dyes are non-toxic and safe
for toys which babies and small children
might chew!

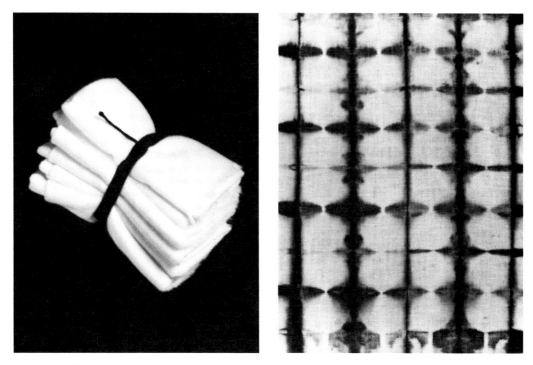

Stripes: Cloth folded in six, pleated and line bound.

Stripes: Cloth folded in half, pleated and open bound with rubber bands.

 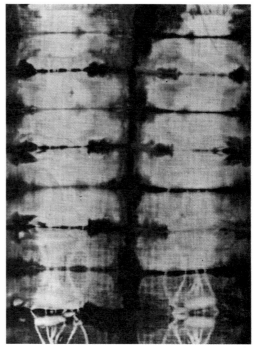

Fabric craft

Practical aprons

illustrated opposite

Father's apron:

Materials
1 plain piece PVC about 35 inches long
by 29 inches wide
2 waist strips 35 inches long by 3 inches
wide
2 shoulder strips 24 inches long by 3
inches wide
1 reel strong white thread
4½ yards white binding
4½ inches Velcro fastener
Strong glue

From the top of the main piece cut away,
from each side, a piece 9 inches wide and
10½ inches deep (diagram 1). Remaining
piece in centre is bib top and these
smaller pieces are for pockets. Fold 1¼
inches to wrong side at top of each
pocket and at top of bib top and machine
this turning in place. With white bias
binding or tape, bind the remainder of
the apron and pockets. Machine the
pockets in place.
Fold narrow turnings to wrong side on
all strips and machine in place. Attach
long strips at either side of waist, and
one end of shorter strips to outer edge of
bib top. Cut Velcro in half and stick one

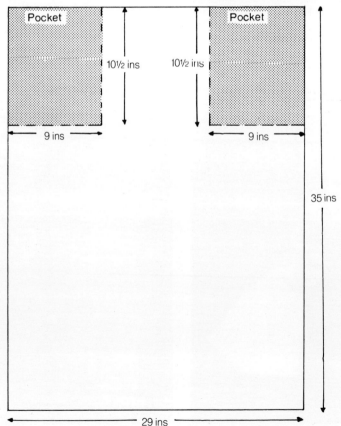

1

Practical aprons, appliqué table set

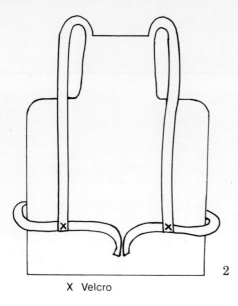

X Velcro

side to wrong side of one end of each short strip, try on apron and stick the other side of Velcro to right side of waist ties so that the shoulder strips, when fastened, fit well (diagram 2).

Mother's apron:

Materials
1 piece PVC 44 inches long by 27 inches wide
2 ties 27 inches long by 3 inches wide
9 inch white bias binding for pocket top
Thread to match PVC and binding

2

Round off the two lower corners of main piece, using plates to guide the curves.

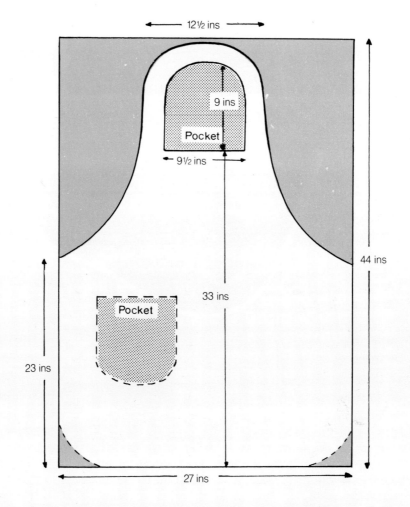

3

Mark 23 inches up from lower edge, at each side, for armholes, then cut away a big curve, using mixing-bowl as guide, from each side in turn, reducing width of bib top to 12½ inches (diagram 3). At 33 inches up from lower edge, slit the centre 9½ inches, leaving 1½ inches at either side: it is better to mark this first on wrong side of work, as it takes pencil marks easily. Mark a spot about 9 inches up from centre of slit. Using mixing bowl as guide, mark a wide curve from this centre spot to either end of the slit, the first few inches from slit ends going almost straight up. This is for the strap which goes round the back of the neck; the cut-away piece becomes the pocket. Now mark on the wrong side the outer edge of the neck strap, 1½ inches away from the inner edge all round and cut, so that there is a continuous neck strap to slip over the head, and pocket. Turn in and machine a very narrow hem all round apron, lower and side edges of pocket, and waist ties except for one short end of each. Bind pocket-top with white binding and machine stitch pocket to apron front; attach ties firmly to either side by unhemmed ends.

Child's apron:

Materials

1 piece PVC about 34½ inches long by 15¾ inches wide
2 waist strips 17 inches long by 1½ inches wide
5 yards bias binding
1 reel matching machine thread
1 scrap contrast PVC
Strong glue
2½ inches Velcro fastener

Round off the two lower corners. 12½ inches up from lower edge, cut away a wide scoop to reduce bib top to 6 inches width, then continue straight up for

outer edges of shoulder straps to end of material. At 17 inches up from lower edge, scoop out a centre curve to leave 1½ inches free at each end; continue this line parallel to outer edge of shoulder straps to end of material. From spare material cut pocket 5 inches by 6 inches. Round off lower edges of pocket. Bind all round apron including shoulder straps; bind top edge of pocket. Turn in tiny hem round remainder of pocket, and round waist ties except for one short end.

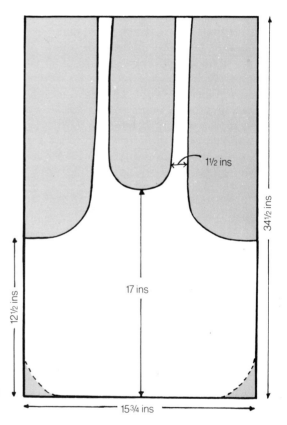

Machine pocket in place; firmly attach waist ties to each side in turn by the unhemmed short end.
From contrast PVC cut appliqué motif of choice, and stick in place. Halve the Velcro and stick in place on shoulder straps and waist ties, as Father's apron.

Appliqué table set

illustrated on page 47

Appliqué is the art of applying one material to another using sewing techniques. It is a wonderful way of using up scraps of dressmaking and furnishing fabrics to good effect and is a most satisfying handicraft. With the technique described here you can work appliqué on many other handmade gifts.

Materials

Even weave fabric for the place mats, patterned or plain. Each place mat measures 17 by $13\frac{1}{2}$ inches. For four place mats you will need 1 yard of 36 inch wide fabric
Cotton fabric for apple shapes, red, pale green and dark green
Heavy non-woven interfacing for napkin rings
$2 \times \frac{3}{4}$-inch button moulds
Matching sewing threads
Stranded embroidery thread

Place mats

To make one mat On the wrong side of the fabric, mark out a rectangle 17 inches wide by $13\frac{1}{2}$ inches deep. Use dressmaker's chalk or a soft pencil. Set the sewing machine to a large sized stitch and machine stich along this line twice. Cut out the table mat, $\frac{1}{2}$ inch outside the stitched line. Unravel the edge and fray back to within two threads of the machine stitching to make a fringed edge. Make three more mats in the same way.

Preparing for appliqué Trace the apple shape and the leaf given on page 53. Draw the apple shape down on to the wrong side of the apple fabric. If you have a swing needle machine, the appliqué can be worked using the zigzag stitch as follows: Set the machine to a narrow zigzag stitch and stitch along the outline on the wrong side of the fabric. Cut out the shape close to the stitching line. Pin and then baste the apple on to the place mat. Set the machine to a wider zigzag stitch and to the smallest stitch length on the machine. Stitch all round the edge of the apple, using a matching thread. Work the apple leaf in the same way and embroider the stem, by hand, in satin stitch.

If you are working the appliqué by hand, draw the apple shape on to the wrong side of the fabric adding $\frac{1}{4}$ inch turnings. Cut out the shape and press the turnings to the wrong side. Baste the turnings and then baste the shape to the background fabric. Stitch the apple shape to the place mat round the edge using either slip stitch or with a closely worked buttonhole stitch. Work the leaf in the same way and embroider the stem in satin stitch.

Napkin rings

To make 1 ring Cut 3 pieces of the table place mat fabric as follows:
1 piece 7 by 3 inches – A
1 piece $6\frac{1}{4}$ by $2\frac{1}{4}$ inches – B
1 piece 3 by $1\frac{1}{4}$ inches – C (button fastener)
Cut 1 piece from interfacing $6\frac{1}{4}$ by $2\frac{1}{4}$ inches – D

Working on piece A, fold and press to the wrong side $\frac{1}{4}$ inch turnings, mitreing the corners neatly. Slip the interfacing piece D under the turnings and baste both materials together.
Working on piece B, turn under and press $\frac{1}{4}$ inch turnings all round, mitreing the corners. Baste and then top stitch $\frac{1}{8}$th inch from the edge.
Working on piece C, fold the fabric along the length and right sides facing. Machine stitch $\frac{1}{2}$ inch from the edge. Turn the fabric inside out and press the 'tube' flat to make loop rouleau.

'His' and 'Her' tidy bag

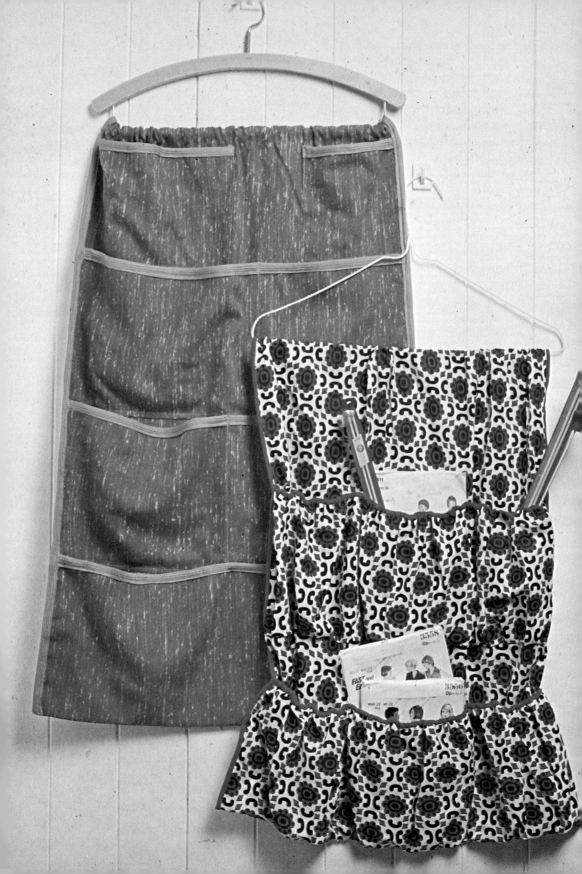

Pin the loop on one short end on the wrong side of the interfaced band with $\frac{3}{4}$ inch of the loop overlapping the edge. Baste and then top stitch the interfaced band, working $\frac{1}{8}$th inch from the edge and catching in the loop.

Place the prepared piece B on the back of the interfaced piece A, wrong sides facing. Baste and then stitch together using small slip stitches and making sure that the stitches do not show through to the right side. Cover a button mould in fabric to match the apple motif. Stitch in position $\frac{1}{2}$ inch from the edge opposite the loop.

'Her' tidy bag

illustrated on page 51

Materials
46 inches of 48 inch furnishing fabric

$3\frac{1}{2}$–4 yards braid
Matching thread
Wooden coat hanger

Cut the main strip 20×40 inches, two pockets 20×8 inches, one 6 inch square and one further piece 6×10 inches. Bind one long top edge of each of these pockets; bind one short end of the long main strip. Fold up this last bound edge to form lowest 8 inch pocket and pin in place; pin the other two pockets immediately above, the lower edge of each coinciding with top edge of pocket below; then pin in place the narrow and the square pockets immediately above third long pocket.

This should leave just sufficient material to fold over the bar of a wooden coat hanger. Machine the lower edges of all

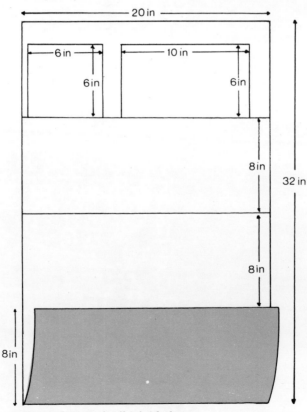

Fabric lay-out for 'his' tidy bag

Appliqué patterns for place mats

pockets in place, and the centre edges of the two smaller top pockets. Pin the side pocket edges to match the side edges of main piece as for woman's tidy bag (the man's has no gathering as the material is stronger). Bind the two long edges. Neaten ends. Sew top edge over bar of coat hanger.

'His' tidy bag

illustrated on page 51

Materials
27 inches of 36 inch patterned cotton without vertical design
3 yards bias binding
Matching thread
Shirring elastic
Wire coat hanger
White enamel paint (optional)

Cut 3 strips 20 inches, 8 inches and 8 inches wide (27 inches long) from cotton fabric. With bias binding and matching thread bind one long edge of each of the two smaller strips. Gather the unbound long edge of each of these strips to a length of 20 inches.
Turn in a small hem along the unbound edges and machine one strip along lower (20 inch) edge of the 27 inch long strip, for the lower pocket, and the other 10 inches up from lower edge for upper pocket. Thread shirring elastic through the binding of each pocket-top. Pin and tack sides of pockets to sides of main strip, and bind the two long edges taking in the pockets along with the main fabric.
Attach the top edge, turning in a hem, to a wire coat hanger, enamelling it white if you prefer before sewing on the pockets. The pockets may be divided by stitching into two or three divisions,

to separate whatever the tidy bag is going to contain.

Beanbags

illustrated opposite

Beanbags make marvellous toys for children and, scaled up, the designs given here could be used to make soft toys or cushions. Use small beans, rice or any of the pulses for filling but remember that the fillings must be emptied out before washing the beanbags. Do not use felt for features if the bags are going to be laundered – use cotton scraps instead.

Materials
Cotton fabric
Felt or cotton scraps
Bean or pulse filling (about 1 lb. for a small beanbag)

Draw out the graph (page 56) and make a paper pattern. Using the paper pattern, cut the shape out of the fabric twice. Cut out eyes, beaks, ears, etc., in felt or cotton fabric. Pin these pieces in position on the right side of one piece of fabric, with the shape lying inwards. Pin and then baste the second piece of fabric on top, right sides facing. Machine stitch all round, leaving an opening of about 2 inches for inserting filling. Pour in the beans, using a paper funnel to make the job easier. Do not overfill or the beanbag loses its effect. Close the opening with closely worked oversewing.

Egg-basket hen

illustrated on page 59

This motherly-looking hen keeps all the breakfast eggs warm – in a basket.

Bean bags

2 *squares* = *1 inch*

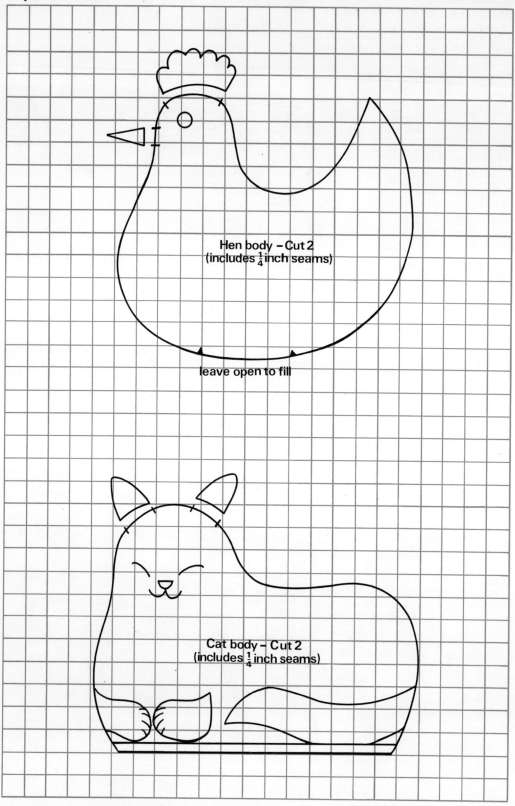

Hen body – Cut 2
(includes $\frac{1}{4}$ inch seams)

leave open to fill

Cat body – Cut 2
(includes $\frac{1}{4}$ inch seams)

Materials

$\frac{1}{2}$ yard patterned cotton fabric
$\frac{1}{2}$ yard matching cotton fabric in plain colour
$\frac{1}{2}$ yard heavyweight non-woven interfacing (or use a piece cut from an old blanket)
Red felt or red fabric for comb and wattle
Yellow felt or cotton fabric for beak
Black felt or cotton fabric for eyes
Matching sewing thread
Kapok stuffing
Matching bias binding
Press stud

(*Follow graph pattern on page 58*).

Cut the hen's body out of the patterned fabric twice, from the lining twice, and from the interlining twice. Cut out the comb, wattle and beak pieces. (If cotton fabric is being used, cut two pieces and seam on the wrong side.) Place two beak pieces together, stitch with stab stitches and stuff.
Lay the comb, wattle and beak on the right side of one head-body piece. Baste in position and place second head-body piece on top, right sides facing. Baste. Stitch along top from point A to B. Turn to right side and stuff hen's head.
Cut linings and interlinings off at the dotted line in pattern, D–E (to give final shape A–D–E–A).
Put one piece of interlining on flat surface. Place one lining on it right side up. Place second lining piece *wrong* side up. Place second interlining piece on top. Baste and seam from A–D–E. Pin lining and interlining into hen, pinning through top fabric as well from A–C–B. Baste. Top stitch for wings on dotted lines of pattern.
Apply bias binding all round hen's body from B–C–A, thus holding lining, interlining and top fabric together.
Catch hen's tail together at C with press stud sewn on inside.

Lining a basket Line the basket with top fabric interlined with a piece of warm blanket.
Trace the base of the basket on to paper. Add $\frac{1}{2}$ inch turnings all round. Measure the circumference of the basket. Double the measurement. Measure the depth from rim to base. Add $2\frac{1}{2}$ inches. Cut a length of top fabric to this measurement. Cut the base shape. Join short ends of the strip on the wrong side. Gather one long edge and pin, baste and stitch to the base piece, pulling up gathers to fit.
Make a $\frac{1}{2}$ inch casing on the other long, raw edge. Insert narrow elastic to fit over the edge of the basket. From the blanket fabric, cut a strip to exactly the circumference of the basket by the depth plus $\frac{1}{2}$ inch. Cut the base shape out with $\frac{1}{2}$ inch turnings. Seam the short ends of the strip. Join the resulting circle to the base piece, pleating to fit. Catch the top fabric to the interlining round the base piece.

Baby Basket

illustrated on page 63

Materials

Mushroom or fruit basket, approx $9\frac{1}{2} \times 6 \times 4$ inches deep
1 yard of 36 inch wide quilted fabric, nylon, cotton or plastic
1 yard of 36 inch wide cotton fabric for lining
1 yard of 11 inch wide white nylon or Terylene fabric
6 yards frilled nylon edging
6 yards of 1 inch wide insert lace
$1\frac{1}{2}$ yards of 4 inch wide lace fabric
3 yards narrow blue ribbon
3 yards narrow pink ribbon
Adhesive
Make a paper pattern for the base of the basket (A), one long side (B) and one short side (C). Cut a strip of quilted fabric, 32 inches long by 5 inches deep,

2 squares = 1 inch

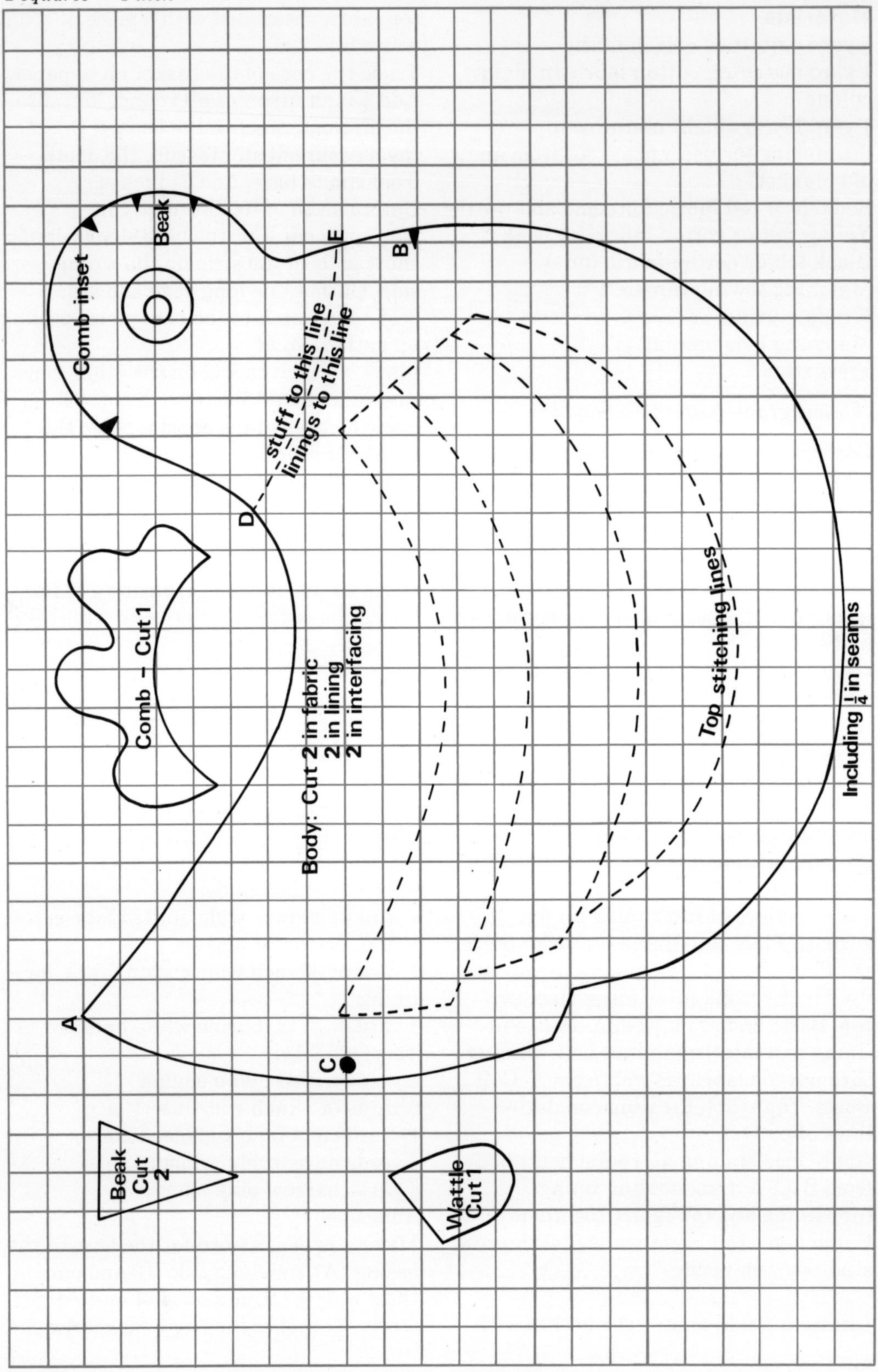

Comb inset

Beak

Comb – Cut 1

stuff to this line
linings to this line

E

B

D

Body: Cut 2 in fabric
2 in lining
2 in interfacing

Top stitching lines

Including ¼ in seams

A

C

Beak
Cut
2

Wattle
Cut 1

Egg-basket hen

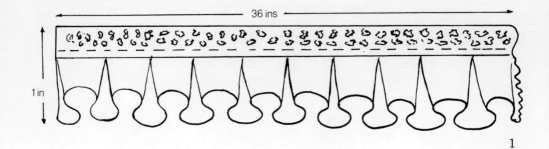

36 ins

1 in

1

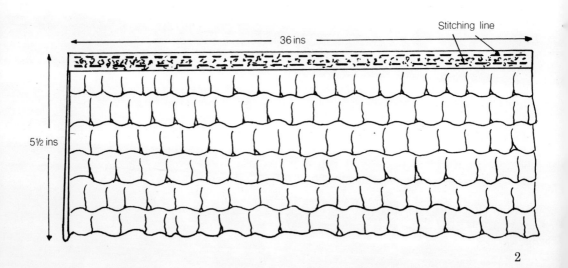

Stitching line

36 ins

5½ ins

2

to line the inner sides of the basket. Stick the quilting to the inside, folding the ends into one corner.

Using pattern A, cut a piece of quilting for the base of the basket, allowing $\frac{1}{2}$ inch turnings all round. Fold in the turnings and glue the lining to the base of the basket.

Pad the outer sides and base of the basket in the same way. Turn and stitch the padded linings at the top edge to neaten.

Next, make a cotton lining for the inside of the basket. Using the paper patterns, cut pieces of the cotton fabric, allowing $\frac{1}{2}$ inch seam allowances all around, as follows: two from pattern B, two from pattern C and one from pattern A. Machine the pieces together to make up the lining, and slip into the basket. Pad the handle of the basket and line with cotton.

Line the outside of the basket in the same way as the inside, but allowing 1 inch seam allowances for the padded thickness of the basket. Pin together the outer cotton lining pieces and check the fit on the basket. Stitch the pieces together and slip this cover over the basket. Turn the raw edges in at the top and slip stitch to neaten.

The nylon cover is then made as follows. Fold the piece of white nylon or Terylene fabric in half lengthwise. Cut 6 lengths of frilled nylon fabric, each 36 inches long and 6 × 36 inch lengths of insert lace. Join each strip of frilled nylon to a strip of lace, along the long edges of each (diagram 1).

Pin, baste and then machine stitch each of these 6 trimming strips to the folded nylon fabric to make 6 overlapping rows (diagram 2).

Wrap this trimmed nylon cover around the basket to fit, then stitch the short ends together. Turn the seam to the inside and slip over the basket. Turn in and stitch the top edge to the basket to secure. Cut approx 12 inches of 4 inch wide lace fabric to cover the handle. Thread pink and blue ribbon through the lace and cover the handle, stitching the trimming to the underside.

Thread ribbons through the remaining lace and hand stitch this around the top of the basket. Use remaining ribbon to make bows at each of the four corners.

Rag doll

illustrated on page 67

Rag dolls are always loved by their owners and you will enjoy making this one for a little girl. She is different from most rag dolls in that her features are delicately embroidered giving her a pert and charming look.

Materials
For the doll, approx. 15 inches tall
$\frac{1}{2}$ yard poplin or Viyella fabric, pale pink or cream

Kapok filling
Anchor stranded embroidery thread, blue
0155, black 0403, deep pink 035, pale
pink 030, white 0402
1 skein Aran knitting yarn for hair
Scraps of pink felt

For the doll's clothes, dress and chemise
½ yard broderie Anglaise with a deep
edging
¾ yard of 1 inch wide broderie Anglaise
insert trimming
½ yard of ½ inch wide cotton lace edging
1½ yards narrow pink baby ribbon
1 press stud

Graph patterns, pages 66–69, include
¼ inch seam allowance

The doll
Draw a paper pattern from the graph
given for the doll's body. Cut out the
head and body piece twice in the pink
or cream fabric. Transfer the features to
head lightly.
Embroider the features, using two
strands of thread throughout. Work the
outer pupil in blue in long and short
stitch. Work the inner pupil in black in
long and short stitch and outline the eye
in stem stitch. Work the white of the eye
in long and short stitch. Outline the
mouth in stem stitch using pale pink.
Work the lower lip in deep pink in satin
stitch and the upper lip in pale pink in
satin stitch. After completing the
embroidery, remove the stuffing from
the head, turn to the wrong side and
press the embroidery lightly. Restuff the
head and neck.
Stitch up the arms and stuff them, firmly
at the hands and wrists, more lightly
near the top of the arms. Oversew the
openings and insert the arms in the
body. Oversew the body turnings on to
the arms. Complete stuffing the body.
Make up the legs and stuff them. Stuff

one piece. Cut out the arm pattern four
times and the leg pattern four times.
Seam the two head and body pieces
together, right sides facing, leaving the
seam open where indicated so that the
arms and legs can be inserted. Stuff the
more lightly at the tops. Oversew the
top openings and insert the legs into the
bottom of the body, keeping the leg
seams to the front. Oversew, using neat
small stitches.
To make up the hair, cut the skein of

Baby basket

yarn through to make one long length and cut a 9 inch length from the bunch for the fringe. Place the bunch on a $9 \times \frac{1}{2}$ inch strip of pink felt so that $2\frac{1}{2}$ inches overlaps the felt, spread the strands out and then machine stitch them to the of felt across the top of the head. Loop the hair back on each side where the ears would be and divide the hair at the back to make side bunches but take care that most of the back of the head is covered.

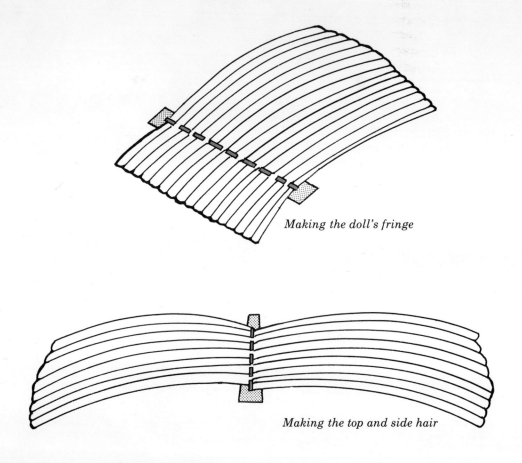

Making the doll's fringe

Making the top and side hair

felt. Pin the felt to the top of the head seam and stitch with small invisible stitches by hand. Trim the fringe if it is necessary just to clear the doll's eyes. Cut the remainder of the skein into two equal lengths and lay them side by side across a strip of felt 4 inches $\times \frac{1}{2}$ inch. Machine stitch along the centre, re-arranging the strands a little so that the felt is hidden along the 'parting'. Turn one short end of the felt under, out of sight, and place this just in front of the top of the head seamline. Stitch the strip

Doll's dress
Following the diagram for the dress pattern, draw out the shape on tracing paper for the measurements given. Cut the dress from the broderie Anglaise twice using the decorative edge for the hem of the dress. Join the shoulder seams first – these are approximately 1 inch wide.
Draw the sleeve pattern out. Cut two sleeves out of the broderie Anglaise and keep the patterned edge of the fabric for the wrist edge. Insert the sleeves into the

64

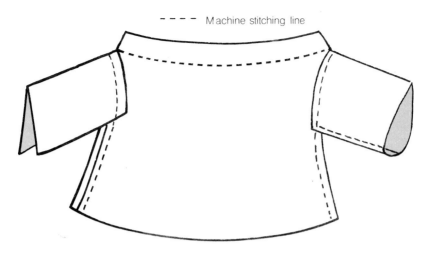

Machine stitching line

Setting in the sleeves and seaming

dress along the shoulder edges. Join the underarm seams of the sleeves. Join the dress side seams.

Make a narrow casing at the neck edge of the dress. Cut a small hole in the casing centre front. Neaten the edges of the hole with buttonhole stitches.

Insert a length of pink ribbon and draw the neckline up to fit the doll.

Doll's chemise

Some plain fabric will remain from the broderie Anglaise. From this, cut the chemise skirt pattern out twice and (*instructions continued on page 70*)

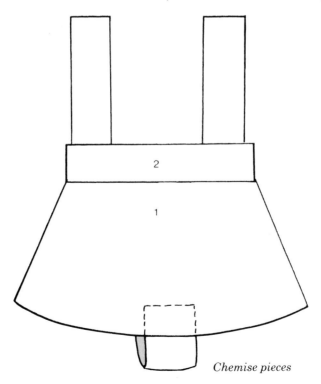

Chemise pieces

2 squares = 1 inch

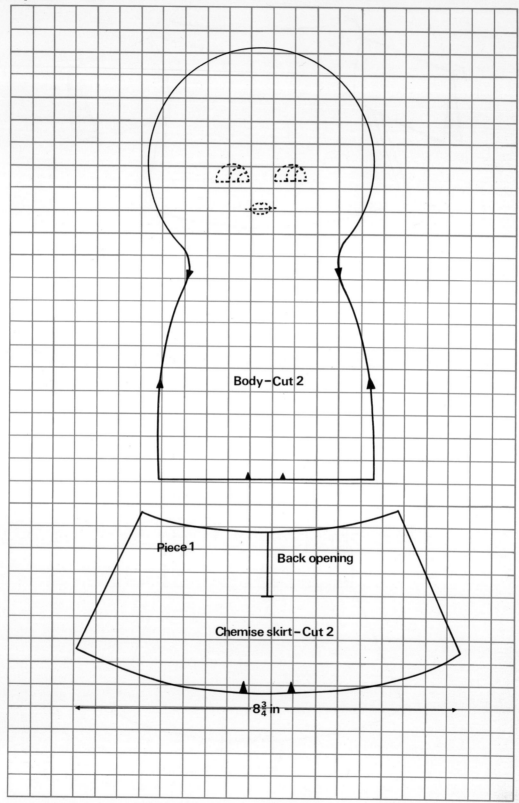

Body – Cut 2

Piece 1

Back opening

Chemise skirt – Cut 2

$8\frac{3}{4}$ in

Rag doll

2 squares = 1 inch

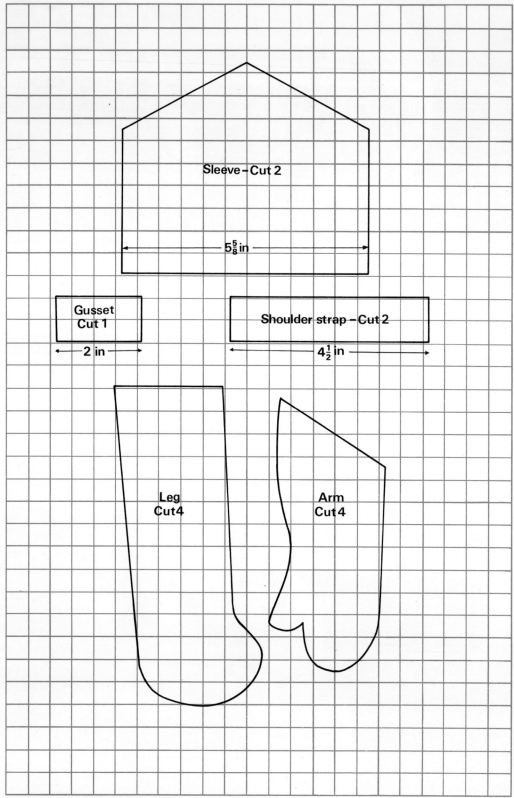

Sleeve – Cut 2

$5\frac{5}{8}$ in

Gusset
Cut 1

Shoulder strap – Cut 2

2 in

$4\frac{1}{2}$ in

Leg
Cut 4

Arm
Cut 4

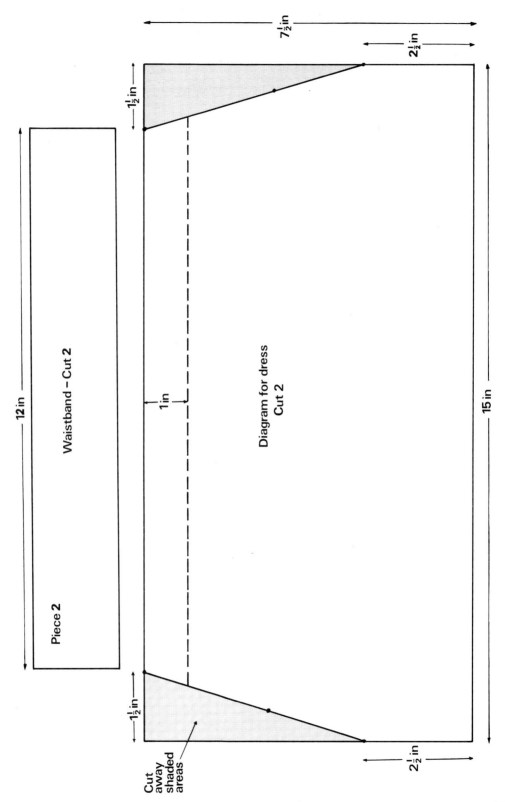

Waistband – Cut 2

Piece 2

12 in

Diagram for dress
Cut 2

7½ in

2½ in

1½ in

1 in

15 in

2½ in

1½ in

Cut
away
shaded
areas

69

slash into one of the pieces for the back waist opening. Neaten this opening by making a narrow hem all round. Join the skirt side seams and trim the hem with the cotton lace edging.

raw edges under once. Finish the back waistband off by turning the raw ends under twice and hemstitching. Stitch a press stud to the back waistband to fasten.

Doll's chemise

Cut shoulder straps, waistband and gusset from the broderie Anglaise insert trimming: the waistband is 12 inches long, the shoulder straps are $4\frac{1}{2}$ inches long each and the gusset 2 inches long. Turn the ends under on the gusset piece and stitch to the wrong side of the back and front skirt hem, just above the lace. Stitch the waistband to the skirt waist, keeping the opening at the skirt back. Stitch the shoulder straps to the waistband at front and back, turning the

Ribbon tray holder

illustrated opposite

Here is a simple yet attractive gift to make for someone setting up a new home perhaps – it is low in cost but high in ingenuity!

Materials
Large sized curtain ring
2 yards wide ribbon or braid

70

Ribbon tray holder

Seam the two short ends of the braid and pass the loop through the ring so that the ends hang at equal length. Lay the braid and ring on a flat surface and move the ends of the loops apart about six inches. Place a pin through the braid just under the ring to hold the angle. Make a few invisible stitches across the four thicknesses, just under the ring to hold the angle. Hang the holder by the ring and one or more trays can be slipped into the loops. The weight of the trays holds them secure.

Cover the ring with thick cotton or string if you prefer.

Felt craft

Felt is a satisfying material to make gifts with because it is comparatively cheap, is available in a wonderful range of colours, requires only very simple sewing techniques and is suitable for embroidery decoration of different types. Felt can be used to make greeting cards, mounted on stiff card, for collage pictures, calendars, pot holders, note book covers and dozens and dozens of other small gifts. The ideas shown here are simple, quick to make and pretty.

Flower pencil tops

illustrated on page 75

Make a little felt flower head to fit on to the end of a pencil and plant six pencils in a flower pot, made from a plastic food pot, for a charming gift for a child or a bazaar.

Materials
Pencils
Felt scraps: yellow, pink, orange, black, lilac, green, white
Matching sewing threads
Small beads
Small plastic pot (e.g. yogurt or cream carton)
Brown felt, 9 inch square
Lump of green plasticine
All-purpose adhesive

Two basic flower shapes are given, one has five petals and the other is a daisy shape. The flower centres are cut from circular patterns in two sizes. The 'stem' pattern is used for both types of flowers.

Petalled flower
Cut out five petal shapes and stitch

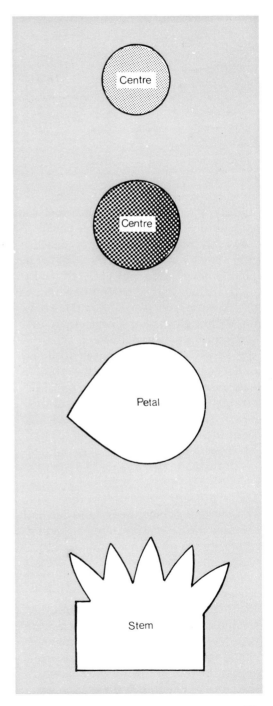

Daisy

where you started and roll it again, this time holding the chalk against the rim of the pot base. This will give you the shape for covering the pot with felt. An all-purpose adhesive is used to glue the felt to the pot. Apply the adhesive just below the rim of the pot and round the rim of the base. Press the felt on to it and join the two long edges with more adhesive. Push a lump of green plasticine into the bottom of the pot. Push the pencils into this at angles to look like growing flowers. You can add the child's name to the pot in cut-out felt letters or in embroidery.

Thimble holders

illustrated opposite

These thimble holders are made in the same way as fabric boxes – that is covering pieces of card with fabric on both sides and joining the covered pieces with an embroidery stitch. The two ends of the holder are pinched together to open the top. The animal designs shown here, a mouse, a rabbit and a fish design are obvious ones to make on the shape but equally pretty holders can be made simply using embroidered patterns or tiny beads and buttons. Work any embroidery or decoration on the fabric before cutting it out. A closely woven fabric should be used for these holders so that there is less likelihood of fraying. Felt works extremely well.

them together at the points. Make a knot on the end of a piece of thread and bring it up through the centre of the flower so that the knot is underneath. Slip a centre circle on to the needle and push it down on to the petals. Slip a bead on to the needle and push it down on to the flower centre piece. Take the needle back through the felt flower centre and the joined petals and finish off the thread with two or three back stitches underneath the flower. Cut the 'stem' pattern out in green felt. Join the short straight edges and try the stem on the pencil to see that it has a close but not tight fit. Stitch the flower head to the 'stem' with matching green thread and small invisible stitches.

Daisy flowers
Cut out daisy flower heads and use both circular flower centres, one on top of the other. Finish off with a bead. Join to the stem as before.

Flower pot
Place the plastic pot on its side on the wrong side of the felt along one straight edge. Hold a piece of chalk against the rim of the pot and slowly roll the pot across the felt, following the rim with the piece of chalk. Put the pot back

Method
Work any surface embroidery or beadwork first. Trace the shape in the diagram overleaf and make a template in stiff card. Using this template cut out 3 shapes in fabric, adding $\frac{1}{4}$ inch turnings and 3 shapes, exactly to the size of the template, in non-woven interfacing for a lining. (Felt can be used for the lining if you prefer.) Using the same template, cut out three more shapes in light card. (The

74

Flower pencil tops, thimble holders, fruit brooches

card from which cereal boxes are made is about the right weight.) Smear fabric adhesive on one side of the card. Place this down on the fabric shape, centring it carefully. Leave to dry. When the adhesive is dry, fold the turnings over – you may need to press them with a cool iron to achieve a good, sharp edge and glue them down on to the card. Work

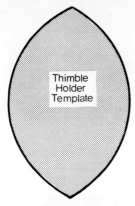

Thimble Holder Template

very slowly and use a sharpened matchstick to apply the adhesive. The smallest spot of adhesive spilt on the fabric will spoil the holder. Press the turnings down firmly with a thumb. Leave to dry. Smear adhesive on the wrong side of the lining and apply it to the card. Press it down firmly and leave to dry. When all three pieces of card have been covered and the adhesive is quite dry, join the three together using Cretan stitch, leaving the top seam open. Add ears, tail and eyes for animal designs.

Fruit brooches

illustrated on page 75

Gay fruit brooches made of brightly coloured and bead-worked felt are lovely gifts for teenagers – they wear them on hats, berets, tote bags; on their shoes and boots, or at the waistline – anywhere in fact where a spot of bright colour is needed.
Patterns for a strawberry, an apple, a

pear, a grape and a carrot are given opposite and on page 78 but you will be able to design others for yourself quite easily once you know how.

Materials
Scraps of felt: scarlet, mauve, purple, lime green, yellow, dark green, orange
Beads for decoration
Anchor stranded embroidery cottons
Cottonwool or kapok for stuffing
Small safety pins

Cut out the pattern shape twice and leaf shapes once. Stitch two fruit shapes together using tiny stab stitches and a matching thread. Leave a gap in the seam for inserting filling. Push cotton wool in using a large darning needle. Close the seam and apply any bead or embroidery required for the character of the fruit or vegetable. Make up the leaves. Stitch to the fruit. Stitch the safety pin to the back of the brooch. The carrot has a green top which is gathered along the base before being attached.
The grapes are gathered into balls and stitched together on the leaf.

Book cover

illustrated on page 79

This is a simple and attractive idea for a gift. Choose a design for the cover which will make it a really personal present.

Materials
Enough felt to go round front, back and spine of chosen book with additional 5 inches on length (for flaps) and 1 inch on height (see diagram on page 80)
Felt scraps in different colours
Trimmings
Stranded embroidery thread

Fold the allowance for flaps (2½ inches at either end) back on to the wrong side.

Trace same size

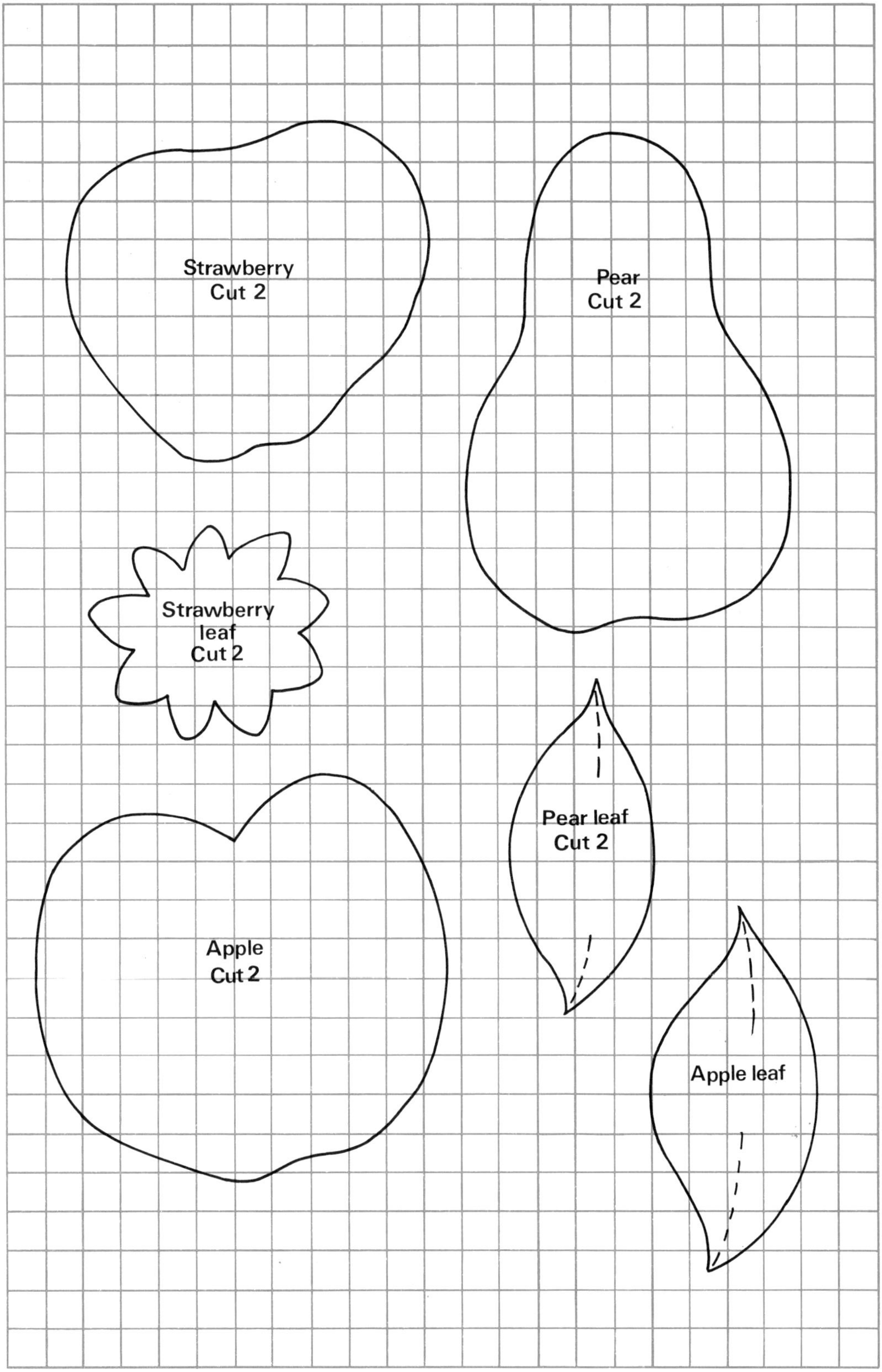

Strawberry
Cut 2

Pear
Cut 2

Strawberry
leaf
Cut 2

Pear leaf
Cut 2

Apple
Cut 2

Apple leaf

Grape
Cut 5

Grape leaf
Cut 1

Stem

Cut to length

Carrot
Cut 2

Carrot top
Cut 1

Gather

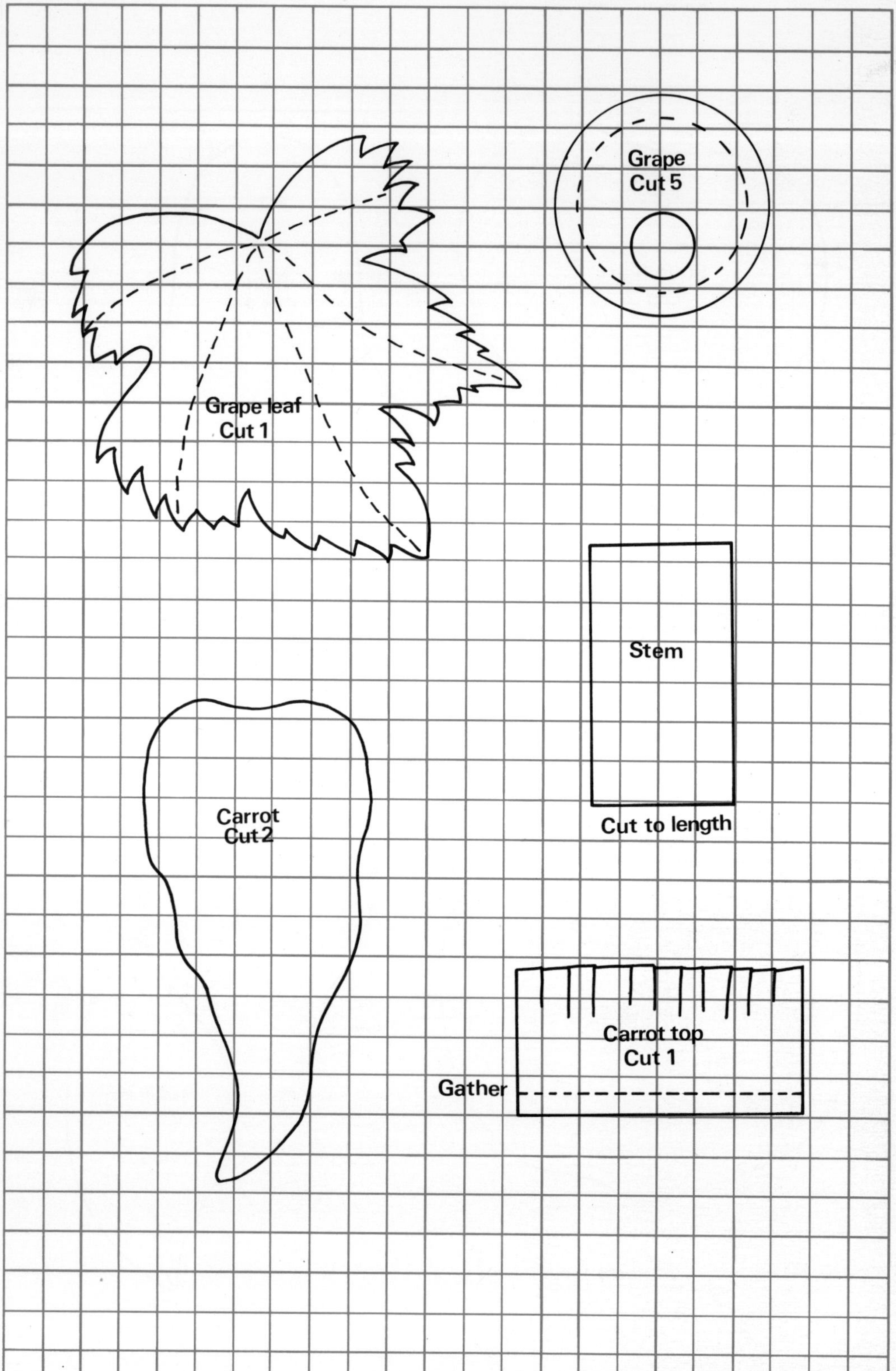

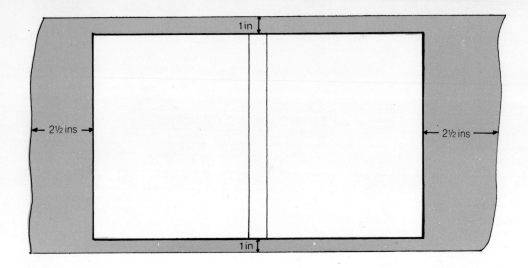

Trace the required design on to the front cover. Trace the design shapes on to the felt scraps. Cut out the felt shapes and position them on the front cover. Sew them very neatly into position, using 2 strands of embroidery thread.

On the book cover illustrated, the scissors and the end of string are embroidered, the scissors in stem stitch and the string in tiny back stitches. Work running stitches $\frac{1}{2}$ inch in from top and bottom edges of book cover, taking the stitches through both thicknesses at the flaps. Using a contrasting colour, whip the running stitches, sewing them always in the same direction.

Decorate the design with trimmings – metallic thread, lace or braid – as required.

Picture

illustrated on page 79

Materials
1 piece yellow linen or textured furnishing fabric, 10$\frac{1}{2}$ by 13 inches
1 piece of felt, 10$\frac{1}{2}$ by 4$\frac{1}{2}$ inches, for conifers
Scraps of felt in three shades, for red roofs and steeple
4 inch square of felt, for shingle
Five shades of larger squares of felt in blue, green and khaki, for mountains
Larger squares of turquoise and white felt, for lake and houses
Matching stranded embroidery thread (use 2 strands at a time)

Trace the design opposite on to the linen, then trace and cut the pieces comprising the design. Fit them together, stitching them very neatly in place. Embroider the windows with tiny straight stitches, those of the church in blue, those of the small left-hand cottage in deep red, and the others in green. Embroider the waterfall in white, filling the area with vertical stem-stitch to give the effect of water. If a piece is too small to cut successfully in felt, such as the eave of the lower centre house, embroider it instead.

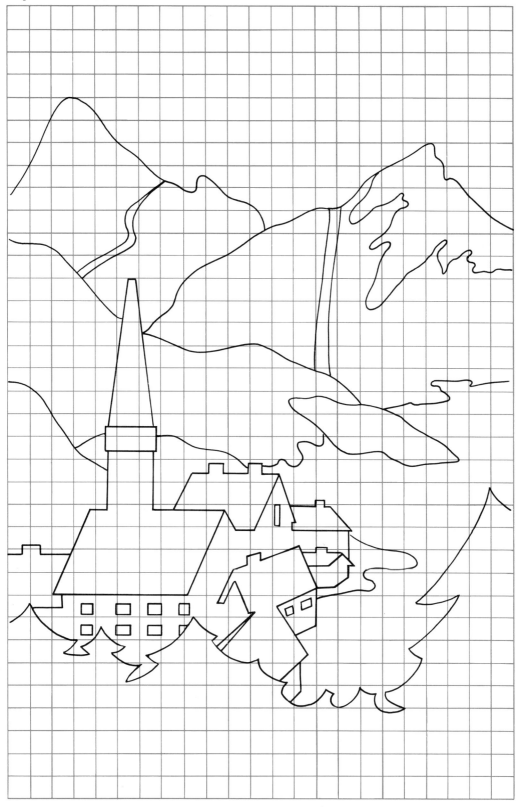

Knitting and Crochet

Baby stockings

illustrated opposite

Materials
Blue Stockings: 2 × 25 gram balls Lister
Baby-Bel Courtelle 4-ply (Fingering
3-ply)
Yellow stockings: 1 oz Patons Beehive
Baby Wool 4-ply (Fingering 3-ply).
¾ yard narrow ribbon
Pair each Nos. 11 (2) and 12 (1) knitting
needles
Note 3 needles would make foot
shaping easier.

Measurements Leg length, 6½ inches;
foot length, 4½ inches

Tension Over patt, unstretched, 7½ sts
and 10½ rows to 1 inch

Abbreviations See page 6.

Both socks are worked alike. With No.
12 (1) needles cast on 44 sts.
1st rib row: K3, *p2, k2; rep from * to
last 5 sts, p2, k3.
2nd rib row: K1, *p2, k2; rep from * to
last 3 sts, p2, k1. Rep these 2 rows 4
times more. Change to No. 11 (2) needles
and patt thus:
1st row: as 1st rib row.
2nd row: K1, p to last st, k1. These 2
rows form patt.

Shape knee Rib 24, ending with k3,
turn, k1, p2, k1, turn, k3, p2, k3, turn, k1,
p10, k1, turn; continue in this way,
working 4 sts more before turning on
every row and keeping in patt, until

'k1, p38, k1' has been worked, then turn
and work across all sts, in patt, until the
shorter side edge measures 5½ inches
from cast-on edge, ending after a 2nd
patt row.

Make Beading *Next row:* k1, *m1, k2
tog, m1, p2 tog, rep from * to last 3 sts,
m1, k2 tog, k1.
Next row: K1, p to last st, k1.

Shape Foot *Next row:* K17, (p2, k2,)
twice, k3, turn, k1, p10, k1, turn; work
in patt across these 12 sts for 12 more
rows for instep. Cut yarn and rejoin it,
right side of work facing, at point of
right needle after the 16 sts already
knitted at ankle; pick up and k10 sts
along nearer side of instep, k the 12 sts
from instep needle, pick up and k10
along other side of instep, then k across
last 16 ankle sts. 64 sts. K11 more rows,
using third needle if necessary, across
these sts.

Shape Heel and Toe *Next row:* K2,
k2 tog, k23, k2 tog, k6, k2 tog, k23, k2
tog, k2. K1 row.
Next row: K2, k2 tog, k22, k2 tog, k4,
k2 tog, k22, k2 tog, k2. K1 row.
Next row: K2, k2 tog, k21, k2 tog, k2,
k2 tog, k21, k2 tog, k2. K1 row. Cast off.

To make up Very neatly join long
centre-back and underfoot seam and
press it, using dry cloth and cool or
rayon-heat iron for Courtelle yarn and
damp cloth and warm iron for wool yarn.
Cut ribbon in half and thread through

*Baby stockings, baby waistcoat, child's
bonnet and scarf*

holes at ankle, tying in neat bow. Make the second stocking in exactly the same way, using the second half of the ribbon for threading through beading.

Knitted caps in pineapple stripes

illustrated on page 91

Instructions are given for the first size. Figures for the larger size, where they differ, are given in brackets.

Materials
2 × 25-gram balls of Sirdar Courtelle Double Knitting (knitting worsted)
Pair each of No. 11 (2) and 9 (4) knitting needles
1 Button (for the smaller size)
2 cardboard circles 1¼ inches in diameter for pompon (for smaller size)

Measurements Around head, 20 inches (22 inches), stretching to fit 22 inches (24 inches); depth from cast-on edge to top, 8½ inches (9¾ inches).

Tension, unstretched, 6 sts and 9 rows to 1 inch.

Abbreviations See page 6.

With No. 11 (2) needles cast on 120 (132) sts. Work 8 (10) rows in k1, p1 rib. Change to No. 9 (4) needles and work pineapple stripe patt thus:
1st row: K1, *p2, k6, p2*, k2, rep from * to *, k1.
2nd row: K3, *p6, k2, p2, k2; rep from * to last 9 sts, p6, k3. Rep these 2 rows once more.
5th row: K1, *p2, twist 3R, twist 3L, p2, k2; rep from * to end, ending with k1.
6th row: K3, *p1, k1, p1, k1, p2, k2, p2, k2; rep from * to last 9 sts, p1, k1, p1, k1, p2, k3.

7th row: K1, *p2, k1, p1, k1, p1, k2, p2, k2, rep from * to end, fin with k1.
8th row: As 6th row.
9th row: As 7th row.
10th row: As 6th row.
11th row: K1, *p2, twist 3L, twist 3R, p2, k2; rep from * ending k1.
12th row: As 2nd row.
These 12 rows form patt. Rep them until 46th (58th) patt row, in all, has been worked.

Shape Top, counting as from 1st row of shaping:
1st row: *K2 tog tbl, p1, twist 3L, twist 3R, p1, k2 tog, rep from * to end, 100 (110) sts.
2nd row: K2, *p6, k1, p2, k1; rep from * to last 8 sts, p6, k2.
3rd row: K1, p1, *k6, p1, k2, p1; rep from * to last 8 sts, k6, p1, k1.
4th row: As 2nd row.
5th row: *K2 tog tbl, k6, k2 tog; rep from * to end. 80 (88) sts.
6th row: K1, p to last st, k1.
7th row: K1, *twist 3R, twist 3L, k2, rep from * to end, ending k1.
8th row: K1, p1, *k2 tog, p2 tog, p4; rep from * ending k2 tog, p2 tog, p1, k1.
9th row: K2, *p1, k5; rep from * to last 4 sts, p1, k3.
10th row: K1, p1, *k1, p5; rep from * to last 4 sts, k1, p2, k1.
11th row: K1, *k2 tog tbl, k2 tog, k2, rep from * to end, ending k1.
12th row: As 6th row.
13th row: *K2 tog, k2 tog tbl; rep from * to end.
14th row: P2 tog across row. Cut yarn, thread through sts, pull tight and fasten off firmly.

To make up Very neatly join side edge for centre-back seam. Press over padded bowl, or wring out a cloth in cold water, lay over cap on bowl and leave until it dries. Sew button to top of larger cap, as there is not enough yarn for a pompon. For the smaller, cut a $\frac{3}{4}$ inch hole in centre of each of the cardboard circles, lay them together, and wind wool over and over the double ring of card until the centre hole is completely filled. Slit along outer edge between the two card rings, tie very tightly between the card circles to bind the threads, then gently pull away the rings and fluff out the pompon; attach it to top of cap by the tie-strings.

Baby waistcoat

illustrated on page 83

This baby waistcoat is based on a French design, 'chauffe-coeur' or 'heart-warmer'. It is quick to make and provides just that fraction of extra warmth for a small baby.

Materials
2×25-gram balls of Lister Baby-Bel Courtelle 4-ply (Fingering 3-ply)
Pair each of Nos. 12 (1) and 10 (3) knitting needles
Small cable needle
4 small buttons

Measurements
To fit chest size 18 inches; mid-shoulder length $8\frac{1}{2}$ inches

Tension
7 sts and 9 rows to 1 inch

Abbreviations
See page 6.

Back
With No. 12 (1) needles cast on 64 sts. Work 10 rows in k1, p1 rib. Change to No. 10 (3) needles.
1st row: Sl1 purlwise, k4, p2, k4, p2, k to last 13, p2, k4, p2, k5.
2nd row: Sl1 purlwise, k6, p4, k2, p to last 13, k2, p4, k7.
3rd row: Sl1 purlwise, k4, p2, c4R, p2, k to last 13, p2, c4L, p2, k5.

4th row: As 2nd row.
These 4 rows form back patt. Cont in patt inc on next and every foll 8th row, inside borders as follows: sl1 purlwise, k4, p2, k4, p2, pick 1k, k to last 13, pick 1k, p2, k4, p2, k5. Continue as indicated until 66th patt row has been completed. 80 sts.

Shape Shoulders Keeping borders as far as possible, cast off 5 sts at beg of next 2 rows, and 6 sts at beg of next 8 rows. Cast off rem 22 sts for back neck.

Left Front
With No. 12 (1) needles cast on 37 sts.
1st rib row: Work 32 sts in k1, p1 rib, k5 for button/buttonhole border.
2nd row: Sl1 purlwise, k5, p1, *k1, p1; rep from * to end. Rep these 2 rows 4 times more: but for a boy, make first buttonhole on next (3rd) row thus: Rib 32, k2, m1, k2 tog, k1.
When 10th welt row has been completed, change to No. 10 (3) needles and work first 4 rows of patt as given for back, with cable panel and borders at both ends. On next and every foll 8th row, 7 times more, work side inc only; making 3 more buttonholes for a boy in front border, on 5th, 17th and 29th rows:
5th row, for a boy, will read: sl1 purlwise, k4, p2, k4, p2, pick 1 k, k to last 13 sts, p2, k4, p2, k2, m1, k2 tog, k1. For 13th row omit buttonhole but work side inc. For 17th row work no side inc but make buttonhole. Do not work buttonholes for a girl. When the 32nd patt row has been completed, 41 sts are on needle.

Front Slope Continuing the side incs where required, begin to shape slope:
33rd row: Sl1 purlwise, k4, p2, k4, p2, k to last 15 sts, k2 tog tbl, p2, k4, p2, k5. Work 3 rows in patt.
37th row: Sl1 purlwise, k4, p2, k4, p2, pick 1 k, k to last 15, k2 tog tbl, p2, k4, p2, k5. Work 3 rows in patt. Rep last 8

rows 3 times more then work 2 more rows, dec. once more inside centre-front border on 65th row: 66 rows, 36 sts.

Shape Shoulder Keeping borders, and dec inside centre-front border once more, cast off thus:
67th row: Cast off 5, p1 more (2 on right needle), c4R, p2, k to last 13, p2, c4L, p2, k5.
68th row: Sl1 purlwise, k6, p4, k2, p to last 8sts, k2, p4, k2.
69th row: Cast off 6, p1 more (2 on needle), k to last 15 sts, k2 tog tbl, p2, k4, p2, k5.
70th row: Sl1 purlwise, k6, p4, k2, p9, k2.
71st row: Cast off 6, k until 5 sts are on right needle, p2, c4L, p2, k5. 18 sts.
72nd row: Sl1 purlwise, k6, p4, k2, p5.
73rd row: Cast off 6, (1 on right needle), k4, p2, k5. 12 sts.
74th row: Sl1 purlwise, k6, p3, p2 tog to stand for last front-slope dec.
75th row: Cast off 6, k to end. 5 sts. For back-neck border cont thus,
76th row: Sl1 purlwise, k4.
77th row: K5. Rep last 2 rows 6 times more, or until this strip, slightly stretched to prevent waviness, reaches halfway along back neck. Cast off.

Right Front
Work to match Left Front, reversing shaping and omitting buttonholes if garment is for a boy, but working buttonholes for a girl. The first row after casting-on will read, sl1 purlwise, k4, *k1, p1; rep from * to end.
2nd row: Rib 32, k5.
Next row, for a girl, will read k2, m1, k2 tog, k1, rib to end; for a boy it will read as 1st row. When 10th welt row has been completed, change to No. 10 (3) needles and work first 4 rows of patt, as given for Back. On 5th and every foll 8th row, patt to last 13 sts, pick 1k, p2, k4, p2, k5. For a girl, make buttonholes on 5th, 17th and 29th patt rows: K2, m1, k2 tog, k1, patt to end, inc before side

border on 5th, 13th, 21st and 29th rows. Complete 32nd patt row. While continuing to inc inside border, start neck slope.
33rd and every foll 4th row: Sl1 purlwise, k4, p2, k4, p2, k2 tog tbl, patt to end. When 67th patt row has been completed, cast off 5 sts once and 6 sts 4 times on next 5 wrong-side rows, while continuing to dec inside front border on 69th and 73rd rows.
77th row: Sl1, purlwise, k4.
78th row: K5. Rep last 2 rows until exactly same length as first neck border. Cast off.

To make up Pin out and press pieces, wrong side facing, with dry cloth and cool or rayon-heat iron for Courtelle. Join shoulder seams and ends of back-neck borders and press. Sew nearer edge of back-neck border very neatly in place and press seam. Join side seams from cast-on edge to end of welt ribbing only, at each side of work, but do not press. Sew on buttons to match buttonholes and darn in all loose ends.

12-section balls in knitting and crochet

illustrated opposite

Materials
Small balls of standard 4-ply yarn in as many colours as possible
Pair of No. 10 (3) knitting needles
No. 3.50 (D/3) crochet hook
Kapok for stuffing

Measurements Knitted ball, about 10 inch circumference; crochet ball, 13 inches

12-section balls, embroidered ball, ball bag

Abbreviations See page 6.

Knitted ball

For each section, with No. 10 (3) needles and working in st-st, cast on 9 sts; inc 1 st at each end of 3rd, 6th and 9th rows, then dec 1 st at each end of 12th row and on every row until 3 sts rem, k3 tog. Fasten off.

Crochet ball

For each section, with 3.50 (D/3) hook, make 9ch, turn.
1st row: Miss 1ch, 8dc(sc) in 8ch. Working in dc(sc), and always turning with 1ch, inc at each end of 2nd, 5th and 8th rows, then dec at each end of 11th row by missing 1dc(sc) at each end, then every row until 2dc(sc) rem. Fasten off.

To make up When 12 knitted or crocheted sections are worked, press them under damp cloth with warm iron. Choose one section as centre and sew one edge of other sections to each of the centre's 5 sides. Similarly treat the other 6 sections; then one cup shape will fit into the other. Join, leaving a space open for stuffing. Stuff with kapok and close last seam.

Embroidered ball

illustrated on page 87

Materials
1 oz each Emu Scotch Double Knitting (knitting worsted) in dark and light colours
Pair of No. 9 (4) knitting needles
Kapok or other stuffing

Measurements 13½ inches circumference

Tension Unstretched, 6 sts and 8 rows to 1 inch

Abbreviations See page 6.

This ball is made in 6 similar sections, of which 3 begin with light colour, changing after 24th row to dark, the other 3 beginning with dark changing to light.
For each section, cast on 1 st.
1st row: K into back, front and back of this st. 3 sts.
2nd row: Inc1, p1, inc1. Working in st-st, inc 1 st at each end of 3rd, 5th, 8th and 12th rows. 13 sts. Work 12 rows straight. Change colours. Work 12 more rows straight. 36 rows.
Dec 1 st at each end of 37th, 41st, 44th, 46th, 47th and 48th rows (the last row being p3 tog).

To make up Pin out pieces, wrong sides facing, and press lightly with warm iron and damp cloth. Embroider on each colour in contrasting shade, in Continental embroidery over 1 st and 2 rows. Insert embroidery needle, threaded with contrasting yarn, from wrong side of work, up at base of a st, insert it two rows up round the back of the st and back into the fabric at the same spot where it emerged, so that it gives the impression of being knitted-in. When the embroidery is completed, very neatly sew together the sections, alternating the colours and leaving a space for stuffing. Stuff. Close seam.

Ball bag

illustrated on page 87

Materials
2 × 25-gram balls of Wendy Invitation Crochet Cotton or any standard 8's cotton crepe

Small quantity of contrast cotton or cord
No. 2.50 (B/1) crochet hook

Measurements The bag will take a 26-inch circumference ball.

Make 7ch, join in ring with sl-st.
1st round: (7ch, 1dc(sc) into ring) 4 times. 4 loops. Always join with sl-st to top of first loop.
2nd round: (7ch, 1dc(sc)) twice into each loop. 8 loops.
3rd round: * (7ch, 1dc(sc)) twice into first loop, once into next loop; rep from * to end. 12 loops.
4th round: (7ch, 1dc(sc)) into every loop.
5th round: * (7ch, 1dc(sc)) twice into first loop, once into each of next 2 loops; rep from * to end. 16 loops.
6th round: As 4th round.
7th round: * (7hc, 1dc(sc)) twice into first loop, once each into next 3 loops; rep from * to end. 20 loops.
8th and 9th rounds: As 4th round.
10th round: * (7ch, 1dc(sc)) twice into first loop, once each into next 4 loops. 24 loops.
11th and 12th rounds: As 4th round.
13th round: * (7ch, 1dc(sc)) twice into first loop, once each into next 5 loops. 28 loops.
Rep 4th round until bag is deep enough to hold ball, allowing for gathering at top; on the last round, crochet 7dc(sc) into each loop to end for firm edge. Fasten off.
For a smaller bag, stop inc at 5th, 7th or 10th rounds and work straight thereafter. For a larger one, work a further inc round on 16th, or 16th and 20th rounds.
With contrast cotton or cord, make a chain long enough to go easily round ball and tie. Thread it through last row of loops then join ends of drawstring so that it cannot be pulled out.

Afghan in Tunisian crochet

illustrated on page 90

Materials
30 ozs Double Knitting (knitting worsted)
No. 5 (0·75 mm) tricot hook

Measurements Afghan is 9 patches wide × 11 patches long. (Enlarge by adding another row of patches to length or width.)

Note Two patches are made from 1 oz. 5 from 2 ozs.

For each patch. With No. 5 (0·75 mm) tricot hook – (a long straight hook with a knob at one end) make 21 ch, miss 1, *draw wool through next ch and retain loop on hook; rep from * to end. 21 loops on hook. Tunisian crochet is always worked on the right side and not turned.
Next row: Wool over hook, draw through first loop, * wool over hook, draw through next 2 loops; rep from * to end: 1 loop on hook.

Tunisian crochet

Next row: *Insert hook from right to left round back, between 1st and 2nd vertical stitch. (Not round the back, but round the single thread.) Draw wool through

page 90: Afghan in Tunisian crochet
page 91: Diagonal cushion

and retain loop on hook; rep with every vertical stitch to end. 21 loops on hook. Rep last 2 rows until 36 rows in all have been completed, or until work is square, finishing with 1 loop on hook.

To cast off Work as for single crochet, inserting hook in each case behind vertical thread, drawing loop through and through loop already on hook, to end of row. 'A row of chain stitches forms the foundation of all Tunisian crochet; a row of single stitches ends it.'

To make up When all patches are completed, pin out and press with a damp cloth and warm iron. Plan the distribution of the colours available, so that the rarer colours are reasonably dispersed and so that a pleasing arrangement results. In general put a dark colour next to a light one. Join the squares alternately side edge to cast-on or cast-off edge. This equalises the pull in wear. Sew all pieces together with matching yarn. Press when completed. Ease in the sides, which may be a fraction longer than top or bottom edge.

Edging
Work 2 rows of dc all round. On the 3rd row, on the longer sides only work *3ch, catch with sl-st into the same dc(sc) as last st, 1dc(sc) into each of next 3dc(sc), rep from * to end, working any left-over dc(sc) in dc(sc). From remaining yarns, cut 10 inch lengths for fringe. Taking 3 at a time, fold them double and knot into each of the 3 ch loops along both sides. Trim fringe.

Diagonal cushion

illustrated on page 91

This diagonally worked cushion is adaptable, in that although the original was worked in rainbow variegated wool,

it would be equally effective worked in stripes using up odd balls. The edging could be applied to other articles.

Materials
8 × 1-oz balls of Lister's Lochinvar Double Knitting (knitting worsted)
2 oz of plain contrast double knitting (knitting worsted) for edging
Pair of No. 8 (5) knitting needles
Cushion pad to fit

Measurements About 17½ inches square, without edging.

Tension 6 stitches and 8 rows to 1 inch.

Abbreviations See page 6.

Begin at one corner of main piece. With main wool cast on 1 st. K twice into this st.
Next row: P1, inc 1 in next st. 3 sts.
Working in st-st, * Inc 1 st at each end of next 3 rows, then work 1 row straight. Rep from * until there are 145 sts on needle, ending with 1 row straight.
**Dec 1 st at each end of next 3 rows, then work 1 row straight. Rep from **until 1 st rems. Fasten off. Work another main piece in same way.

Edging
With contrast wool, cast on 3 sts.
1st row: Sl1 purlwise, inc 1, k to end.
2nd row: K to last 2 sts, inc 1, k1. Rep these 2 rows 3 times more. 11 sts.
9th row: Sl1 purlwise, k2 tog, k to end.
10th row: K to last 3 sts, k2 tog, k1. Rep last 2 rows until 3 sts rem. Rep last 16 rows until straight edge measures 70 inches or 178 centimetres, or is long enough to fit around all 4 sides of cushion, ending after a 16th row. Leave these sts on holder for adjustment, either to add to or undo 16 rows as required.

To make up Pin out the two squares,

wrong side facing, and press lightly with warm iron and damp cloth. Join very neatly round 3 sides, insert cushion pad and close 4th side. Very neatly sew edging all round by straight edge, firm off the last sts when required.

Knitted tie

illustrated on page 95

Materials
1 × 50-gram ball of Patons Purple Heather 4-ply (Fingering 3-ply)
Pair of No. 11 (2) knitting needles

Measurements Width at broadest part, $2\frac{3}{4}$ inches; at narrowest, $1\frac{3}{8}$ inches; length, 51 inches.

Tension 7 stitches and 11 rows to 1 inch.

Abbreviations See page 6.

The tie is worked entirely in moss st and depends for its effect on the rainbow or random dye yarn.
Cast on 1 st.
1st row: (K1, p1, k1) into this st.
2nd row: K1, p1, k1.
3rd row: Inc in each of first 2 sts, k1. 5 sts.
4th row: K2, p1, k1, k1.
5th row: Inc in first st, k1, p1, inc in next st, k1. 7 sts.
6th row: K1, *p1, k1; rep from * to end.
7th row: Inc in first st, *p1, k1; rep from * to last 2 sts, inc in next st, k1, 9 sts.
8th row: K2, *p1, k1; rep from * to last st, k1.
9th row: Inc in first st, *k1, p1; rep from * to last 2 sts, inc in next st, k1. 9 sts.
10th row: As 6th row. Rep last 4 rows

until there are 19 sts or until tie measures required width.
Continue straight in moss st until tie measures 18 inches from point.
1st dec row: K2 tog tbl, *k1, p1; rep from * to last 3 sts, k1, k2 tog. 17 sts.
Next 17 rows: As 6th row.
2nd dec row: K2 tog tbl, p1, *k1, p1; rep from * to last 2 sts, k2 tog. 15 sts.
Next 17 rows: As 6th row. Rep last 36 rows, from 1st dec row, until 9 sts rem, then continue straight, always as 6th row, until tie measures 51 inches or required length. Cast off.

To make up Darn in any loose ends; press lightly with damp cloth and warm iron.

Crochet tie

illustrated on page 95

Materials
1 oz Wendy 4-ply Nylonized wool (Fingering 3-ply) in each of two colours
No. 3.00 (C/2) crochet hook

Measurements Width at widest part, 3 inches; at narrowest, $1\frac{5}{8}$ inches; length, $52\frac{1}{2}$ inches

Tension $6\frac{1}{2}$ stitches and 7 rows to 1 inch, measured on the straight.

Abbreviations See page 6.

Note The yarn must be darned in every 2 rows as it cannot be carried up along the side. When changing colours, leave only a short end to be darned, to avoid extra bulk.

With dark wool make 30 ch.
1st row: Turn, miss 1, 2dc(sc) into next

ch, 1dc(sc) into each of next 12ch, miss 1, 1dc(sc) in next ch, miss 1, 1dc(sc) into each of next 12 ch, 2dc(sc) into last ch.
2nd row: 1ch, 2dc(sc) into first dc(sc), 1dc(sc) into each of next 12dc(sc), miss 1, 1dc(sc), miss 1, 1dc(sc) into each of next 12dc(sc), 2dc(sc) into last dc(sc). This last row forms patt. Rep patt row, working 2 rows in light then 2 rows in dark, alternately, throughout.
When the 36th patt row (light) has been completed, begin shaping thus:
37th row: (dark), 1ch, 1dc(sc) into each of next 13dc(sc), miss 1, 1dc(sc), miss 1, 13dc(sc) (no incs at either end) (27dc(sc)).
38th and foll rows: 1ch, 2dc(sc) into first dc(sc), 11dc(sc), miss 1, 1dc(sc), miss 1, 11dc(sc), 2dc(sc) into last dc(sc).
When the 68th patt row has been completed from beginning,
69th row: (dark) 1ch, 12dc(sc), miss 1, 1dc(sc), miss 1, 12dc(sc). (25dc(sc)).
70th and foll rows: 1ch, 2dc(sc) in first dc(sc), 10dc(sc), miss 1, 1dc(sc), miss 1, 10dc(sc), 2dc(sc) in last dc(sc). When 80th patt row from start has been completed,
81st row: (dark) 1ch, 11dc(sc), miss 1, 1dc(sc), miss 1, 11dc(sc). (23dc(sc)).
82nd to 92nd rows: 1ch, 2dc(sc) in first dc(sc), 9dc(sc), miss 1, 1dc(sc), miss 1, 9dc(sc), 2dc(sc) into last dc(sc).
93rd row: (dark) 1ch, 10dc(sc), miss 1, 1dc(sc), miss 1, 10dc(sc). (21dc(sc)).
94th to 100th rows: 1ch, 2dc(sc) into first dc(sc), 8dc(sc), miss 1, 1dc(sc), miss 1, 8dc(sc), 2dc(sc) into last dc(sc).
101st row: (dark) 1ch, 9dc(sc), miss 1, 1dc(sc), miss 1, 9dc(sc). (19dc(sc)).
102nd to 108th rows: 1ch, 2dc(sc) into first dc(sc), 7dc(sc), miss 1, 1dc(sc), miss 1, 7dc(sc), 2dc(sc) into last dc(sc).
109th row: (dark) 1ch, 8dc(sc), miss 1, 1dc(sc), miss 1, 8dc(sc). (17dc(sc)).
110th to 116th rows: 1ch, 2dc(sc) into first dc(sc), 6dc(sc), miss 1, 1dc(sc), miss 1, 6dc(sc), 2dc(sc) into last dc(sc).
117th row: (dark) 1ch, 7dc(sc), miss 1, 1dc(sc), miss 1, 7dc(sc). (15dc(sc)).
118th to 124th rows: 1ch, 2dc(sc) into

first dc(sc), 5dc(sc), miss 1, 1dc(sc), miss 1, 5dc(sc), 2dc(sc) into last dc(sc).
125th row: (dark) 1ch, 6dc(sc), miss 1, 1dc(sc), miss 1, 6dc(sc). (13dc(sc)).
126th to 132nd rows: 1ch, 2dc(sc) into first dc(sc), 4dc(sc), miss 1, 1dc(sc), miss 1, 4dc(sc), 2dc(sc) into last dc(sc).
133rd row: (dark) 1ch, 5dc(sc), miss 1, 1dc(sc), miss 1, 5dc(sc). (11dc(sc), 11 st).
This completes tie shaping, until last few rows.
134th and foll rows: 1ch, 2dc(sc) into first dc(sc), 3dc(sc), miss 1, 1dc(sc), miss 1, 3dc(sc), 2dc(sc) into last dc(sc).
Cont thus, until 268th row has been completed, or until tie measures required length, ending after a 4th colour patt row.

Shape End Keeping colours correct.
Next row: 1ch, 4dc(sc), miss 1, 1dc(sc), miss 1, 4dc(sc).
Next row: 1ch, 3dc(sc), miss 1, 1dc(sc), miss 1, 3dc(sc).
Next row: 1ch, 2dc(sc), miss 1, 1dc(sc), miss 1, 2dc(sc).
Next row: 1ch, 1dc(sc), miss 1, 1dc(sc), miss 1, 1dc(sc). (3dc(sc)). Break wool and fasten off.

To make up Darn in all loose ends. Press lightly with damp cloth and warm iron.

Child's bonnet and scarf

illustrated on page 83

Materials
3 ozs of Wendy Nylonised 4-ply in yellow
Small ball of above wool in blue
Pair each of Nos 10 (3) and 11(2) knitting needles

Knitted and crochet ties

Measurements
Bonnet: round face edge: 16 inches
Scarf: 31½ inches long

Tension
About 7 sts and 9 rows to 1 inch over st-st

Abbreviations
See page 6.

Scarf
This is made in two similar pieces, joined at centre-back. For each piece, with No. 10 (3) needles and yellow cast on 41 sts.

1st row: K.

2nd row: Sl1, purlwise, k to end. Rep 2nd row 8 times more.

Begin patt: 1st row: As 2nd border row.

2nd row: Sl1 purlwise, k4, p to last 5 sts, k5. Rep these 2 rows once more.

5th row: Sl1 purlwise, k4, in yellow; join blue without cutting yellow and in blue (k3, put right needle into same st (that is last of 3k sts) *4 rows down* and pull loop through, put loop on point of left needle and k it tog tbl with next st – called k1 below – if you do not k the sts tog tbl, the contrast colour would be lost) rep to last 8 sts, k3; drop blue, join on another ball of yellow and k last 5 sts.

6th row: Yellow, Sl1 purlwise, k4, twist wools (lay one yarn over the other at back of work) and with blue p to last 5 sts, twist wools, k5 yellow.

7th row: With yellow, sl1 purlwise, k4, twist wools, k in blue to last 5 sts, twist wools, k5.

8th row: As 6th row.

9th row: Drop blue and second ball of yellow, and using first ball of yellow, slip 1 purlwise, k5; *k1 below, k3; rep from * ending k1 below, k6.

10th, 11th and 12th rows: As 2nd, 1st and 2nd rows.

The last 8 rows form patt. (4 rows alternately in blue and yellow, always with yellow border.) Rep patt until 36th patt row has been completed. Discard blue and second ball of yellow for the meantime.

Begin shaping
37th row: Slip 1 purlwise, k3, k2 tog, k to last 6 sts, k2 tog, k4.

38th, 39th and 40th rows: As 2nd, 1st and 2nd rows. Rep. last 4 rows until 21 sts rem. Work 3 rows after the last decs. Change to No. 11 [2] needles and k1, p1 rib, beg and ending alt rows either with k2, for neat knotted edge, or with p1 to keep rib right, until this half of scarf measures 15¾ inches long from cast-on edge, ending after a wrong-side row. Cast off in rib. Make another piece in exactly the same way.

Bonnet
With No. 10 (3) needles and yellow cast on 97 sts, and work exactly as for beg of scarf, for 28 patt rows in all, ending after a yellow stripe. Cut blue and second ball of yellow and reverse work, so that brim will fold over on to right side.

29th row: K1, p to last st, k1. Now working in st-st, cont without shaping until 6 inches of st-st have been worked, ending after a p row. Cast off 32 sts on each of next 2 rows. Work 4 rows without shaping on centre 33 sts, then dec 1 st at each end of next and every following 4th row, until 17 sts rem. Cont without shaping if necessary, until side edge of this part from the cast-off sets of 32 sts measures same length as cast-off 32. Cast off.

To make up Pin out pieces, with wrong side facing, to required measurements and press lightly with warm iron and damp cloth, avoiding the ribbing. Very neatly join the cast-off scarf ends and press seam lightly. Very neatly sew side extensions of bonnet to nearer set of cast-off sts, at each side of work, and press seams. Fold back brim on to right side of work and catch in place at sides. Sew the bonnet to the scarf, slightly gathering the lower edge of bonnet into the ribbed part and leaving about 24 rows of ribbing free at each end to tie. Press join.

Hut slippers

illustrated on page 99

Materials
3 ozs of Lister Lochinvar Double Knitting (knitting worsted)
Pair each of Nos 11 (2) and 9 (4) knitting needles
Pair of soles, size 5–6 or 10 inches long

Tension 6 sts and 8 rows to 1 inch

Abbreviations See page 6.

Both slipper-tops are worked alike. For each, with No. 11 (2) needles cast on 52 sts. Work 36 rows (4½ inches) in k1, p1 rib, inc 1 st in centre of last row. Break yarn. Sl 13 sts from each end of needle on to holders and rejoin yarn, right side of work facing, to centre 27 sts. Change to No. 9 (4) needles and st-st and work 52 rows straight. (6½ inches.) Then dec 1 st at each end of next and every alt row until 11 sts rem. Work 1 row after last decs. Cast off.
Very neatly join side edges of ribbed piece for back seam. With right side of work facing, rejoin wool to 26 heel sts and with No. 9 (4) needles and working in st-st, inc 1 st at each end of 1st and every alt row foll until there are 44 sts. Work 1 more row. Cast off.

To make up Press instep piece and heel piece lightly with damp cloth and warm iron. Sew shaped edges to heel piece neatly along side edges of instep piece as far as they go without stretching. Press seams. Sew slipper-top to sole.

Junior hut slippers

illustrated on page 99

Materials
1 oz Wendy Nylonised 4-ply in each of red and white
Pair each of Nos. 12 (1) and 10 (3) knitting needles
Pair of soles, size 11–12 or 8 inches long

Tension About 7 sts and 9 rows to 1 inch

Abbreviations See page 6.

Both slipper-tops are worked alike. For each, with No. 12 (1) needles and red wool cast on 47 sts. Work 28 rows in k1, p1 rib, beg and ending alt rows with either k2, for neat knotted edge, or p1, to keep rib right, and making beading thus on *7th* and *21st rows:* K1, *m1, k2 tog; rep from * to end.
Break wool. Sl first 10, and last 10 sts on to holders. With No. 10 (3) needles work in st-st, on centre 27 sts, thus. Join white without breaking red.
Rows 1, 2, 3 and 4: 3 red, *3 white, 3 red; rep from * to end.
Rows 5, 6, 7 and 8: 3 white, *3 red, 3 white; rep from * to end. These 8 rows form patt. Rep them 4 times more then rows 1 to 4 once. Cut white. Working in red st-st, dec 1 st at each end of next and every row until 11 sts rem. Work 1 more row. Cast off.
Very neatly join sides of ribbed piece to form centre-back seam. Join red wool to 20 heel sts. With No. 10 (3) needles and working in st-st, inc 1 st at each end of 1st and every alt row foll until 40 sts are on needle. Work 1 more row. Cast off.

To make up Press instep piece and heel piece lightly with warm iron and damp cloth. Sew shaped edges of heel piece neatly along side edges of instep piece as far as they go without stretching. Press seams. Sew slipper top to sole. For ankle ties, use either cord, ribbon or crochet chain; fold ribbing in half to right side so that beadings coincide. Thread ties through holes.

Hut slippers

Embroidery

Pillow cover

illustrated on page 103

Materials
1 piece black and red tweed or fairly
thick fabric, 18 by 16 inches
1 skein each black and red Patons
Turkey Rug wool
3 skeins, 2 in black and 1 in red stranded
embroidery thread
16 inch zip fastener
Matching thread

Trim the cut edges, making sure they
are perfectly straight. Fold the material
exactly in half, pin or tack along
halfway fold, then open out material and
draw the design on one half. With a
ruler or straight piece of wood draw two
lines, 1 inch apart, in the centre, and
other lines parallel to and about $\frac{1}{2}$ inch
apart. Against the outer lines place one
bowl or plate in centre with a smaller
one either side, at each side of work in
turn, and draw round them to form the
semi-circular scallop shapes, again
drawing other lines $\frac{1}{2}$ inch beyond round
the curves. This forms centre motif.
Similarly, either side of centre motif and
using same methods, draw single
parallel lines fully 1 inch apart and
about $8\frac{1}{2}$ inches away from the centre
lines at either side, and draw single
curves, the larger in the centre and
smaller ones at either side. Using three
strands of the embroidery thread at a
time, in matching colours, couch down
the four centre lines with black rug
wool: this means simply laying the wool
from one end to the other, and catching
it very neatly in place every $\frac{1}{4}$ inch with
the stranded cotton. Now couch a line

of red rug wool between each pair of
black centre lines. Couch red rug wool
round the centre pair of curves,
couching black wool as a sandwich
between them. For the outer motifs,
couch the two centre lines at each side
in red rug wool, and the curves in black
rug wool.
When the embroidery is completed, fold
the material right side in and machine
along the two long sides. Turn right side
out and sew in zip fastener, neatening
the ends.

Edging
To make the edging mark off, with pins,
along all four sides of the embroidered
half, every 2 inches. Starting at one
corner, couch down black wool all along
seams and fold, and at every pin mark,
loop the wool round your left forefinger,
catching this loop firmly in place: repeat
this all round.

Purse

illustrated on page 111

A pretty change purse makes a charming
gift and particularly when you have
embroidered it yourself. Purse frames
are obtainable from most large
department stores and needlework shops,
or you may find a beautiful antique
frame on a worn out purse in a junk
shop. Simply cut the worn purse away
and stitch a new purse to the old frame.

Materials
$2\frac{1}{4}$ inch wide purse frame

Pink evenweave fabric 14 by 8 inches
Matching lining fabric
Matching Drima thread
Non-woven interlining
Anchor stranded embroidery cotton,
Almond Green 0263; Muscat Green 0279;
Buttercup 0298; White 0402

Cut the fabric into two pieces, each
7 × 5 inches. Transfer the design
(diagram 1) on to one piece of the fabric

and work the design following the key
for colours and stitches.
When the embroidery is completed, press
the wrong side lightly. Make a pattern
following diagram overleaf and cut the
shape from the embroidered fabric and
from the piece of unembroidered fabric.
Cut the shape from the interlining twice.
Cut the shape from the lining fabric
twice. Place the interlinings on the
wrong sides of the two pieces of top

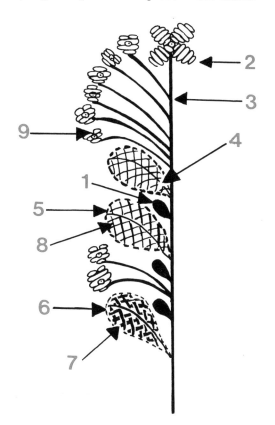

1

Key to embroidered purse motif

1	0263	Satin stitch	6	0279	Back stitch
2	0402	Satin stitch	7	0263	Herringbone stitch
3	0263	Stem stitch	8	0279	Herringbone stitch
4	0279	Stem stitch	9	0298	French knots
5	0263	Back stitch			

Trace same size

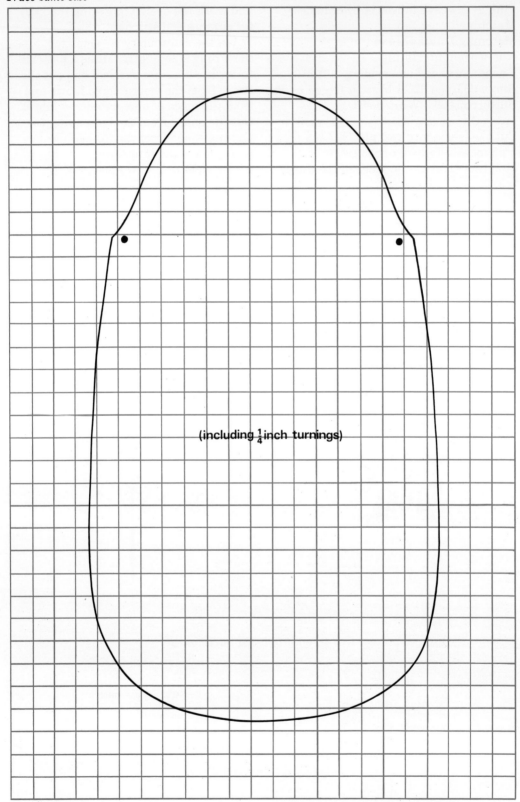

(including $\frac{1}{4}$ inch turnings)

Pillow cover, needlepoint pin cushion

fabric and making up as one, seam the two purse pieces together from ● to ●, right sides facing. Press the seam first flat and then open. Trim the seam and clip into the curves. Turn to the right side. The purse is attached to the frame as follows: pin and then baste the top of the purse to the frame. (You will find it easier to push pins through the holes in the frame to hold the fabric while you are basting.) Turn in ¼ inch of the fabric at the mouth of the purse and baste the fabric to the frame lightly, taking the basting stitches through the small holes in the purse frame. Make small oversewing stitches to secure the fabric to the frame, taking one stitch through every frame hole. Remove the basting stitches. Finish the edge with oversewing stitches in Muscat Green as illustrated. Make up the lining, right sides facing and trim the seam. Slip the lining into the purse and make a ¼ inch turning on the mouth of the purse lining. Slip stitch into position.

Florentine spectacles case

illustrated on page 107

This beautiful canvas work spectacles case is worked in a zigzag stitch called 'flame' and is one of the Florentine or Bargello patterns. For this kind of needlework the yarn colours must be chosen carefully to achieve the brilliant effect which is typical of Florentine embroidery. The colours should range from light to dark in a closely related scheme with one sharp or strongly contrasted colour. Florentine embroidery, which is amazingly quick to do, can be used to make a variety of acceptable accessory gifts, from belts and hairbands to handbags and smaller items.

Materials
12 by 12 inches single weave canvas, 16 threads to the inch.
1 skein Anchor tapisserie wool in each of the following colours: Cream 0366; Sand 0347; Amber 0427; Orange 0333; Brown 0379; Maroon 071
12 by 12 inches brown lining silk
1 skein Anchor stranded embroidery thread Cinnamon 0371
Tapestry needle
Embroidery needle

Draw out the shape of the case (opposite) and trace it on to the canvas, using either dark coloured water colour paint and a brush or a felt-tipped pen. Choose any of the colours for the foundation row and following the chart (diagram 1) work one row of the pattern right across the canvas from side to side of the case.

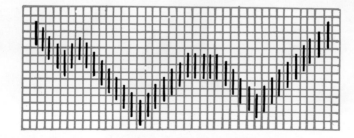

1

2 squares = 1 inch

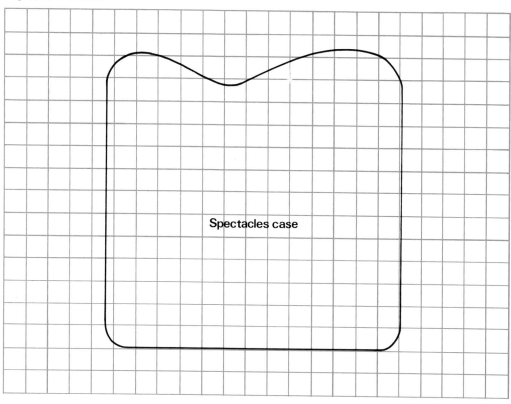

Spectacles case

You will find that you will work just over three repeats. Each stitch is worked over three threads of canvas. Once you have worked this foundation row it is a simple matter to work the rest of the pattern, changing to the next colour for each row. The flame pattern illustrated uses the yarn colours in the following order: cream, sand, amber, orange, brown and maroon.

When the embroidery reaches the edges of the outlined shape you will find that, to follow the curves, you may have to work over two or even a single thread. This is acceptable, as long as you keep to the order of the colours in the pattern.

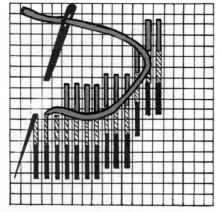

Florentine stitch

To make up When the embroidery is completed, stretch the canvas as follows: lay two or three thicknesses of blotting paper on a board and dampen the paper thoroughly. Place the embroidery face upwards on the dampened paper and using drawing pins, pin the work to the board, working from the centre of the top edge and outwards. Leave until the paper has dried out.

Unpin the canvas and trim the excess canvas away to within ½ inch of the embroidery. Fold the turnings to the wrong side and baste. It may be necessary to clip into the top edge curve to make the canvas fold more easily.

Make sure that no unworked canvas shows on the folded edge – if stitches have been missed out, this is the point at which they should be worked. Cut the lining fabric to match the trimmed canvas size and turn the ½ inch turnings to the wrong side. Press and then baste the lining to the wrong side of the canvas work, matching straight edges. Slip stitch all round.

Fold the spectacle case down the middle, matching the sides and oversew the long side and across the bottom with tiny, neat stitches.

Finish off these edges with Cretan stitch, worked in the stranded embroidery thread.

Needlepoint pin cushion

illustrated on page 103

Materials
Of double thread canvas, 10 threads to the inch:
   1 piece 5 inches square
   1 piece 13 by 2½ inches
Of Anchor stranded cotton:
   3 skeins in white
   2 skeins in each of black, poppy red, golden brown
4½ inches of 36 inch wide lining material
Matching thread for lining
4½ inch square of red felt
Matching red thread
Stuffing

Working from the chart, count 4 rows in from each edge, for turnings, before beginning the work. Tack a line down the centre of the canvas square, and work from the centre out. Use 6 strands of thread and work in simple cross-stitch, always keeping the upper stitch slanting in the same direction – upwards from right to left.

106

Florentine spectacles case

When the circle is completed, work the surrounding band. As the stitch repeat is only 2, the length can easily be adjusted. The original band was 120 threads long, and 17 threads deep.

To make up When both pieces are finished, press them gently with a warm iron and a damp cloth. Trim round the circle leaving an unworked border about 4 threads deep for turnings. Cut 2 corresponding circles and one matching long strip from lining material. Form the long canvas work strip into a ring; fold the top turning to wrong side of work and buttonhole stitch in red along this top edge. Buttonhole stitch in black all round canvas work circle. Fit them in place and whip them together with the golden-brown thread. Make up the lining from the two circles (for top and

/ = Black
X = Red
O = Gold

Chart for surrounding band

Pin cushion top: 39 stitches across
39 rows deep

108

base) and the encircling strip, leaving a small opening for inserting the stuffing. Insert stuffing and close the opening. Fit this pad inside the canvas work, keeping out the unworked canvas edges of the surrounding strip. Turn these back and lace them together, criss-cross, evenly over base of pad. Cut the red felt to match base circle and stitch very firmly in place.

Check cushion

illustrated on page 111

Checked material makes an interesting background for embroidery. The measurements given below are for the cushion illustrated but the instructions are easily adapted to suit any material. *See pages 109–113 for stitch diagrams.*

Materials
Piece of black and white needlecord 33 by 53 inches. (Cushion top will be 16½ by 26½ inches.)
Turquoise felt for circles
Matching turquoise thread
Anchor stranded thread in coral, black and white
Ric-rac or Vandyke braid to match felt
½ yard press stud tape

Cut out 12 circles from felt using a compass or drawing round base of a wine glass. Stitch one circle into each square of top of cushion, using matching thread. Using embroidery thread work a different pattern in each circle using coral, black and white. The circles in this cushion are filled as follows: Solid flystitch, two quarters in white and one quarter each in the other two colours; two curved segments, coral and white, in Roumanian stitch; two herringboned lines in right angles in black and coral with white star stitches between; stem stitch; wheatear stitch; back stitch; buttonhole-stitch and spider's web

filling. These circles can be filled to make a sample of stitches of your choice taken from a standard embroidery book.

To make up Fold the material in half. Seam each short end. Seam the remaining opening for 3½ inches at each end leaving central opening for inserting cushion. Turn in a small hem on each side of opening. Sew in press stud tape. Sew ric-rac braid all round top of cushion, ½ inch in from outer edge.

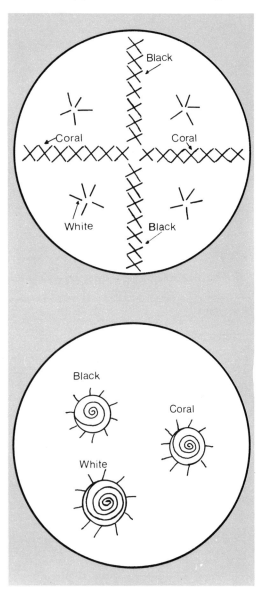

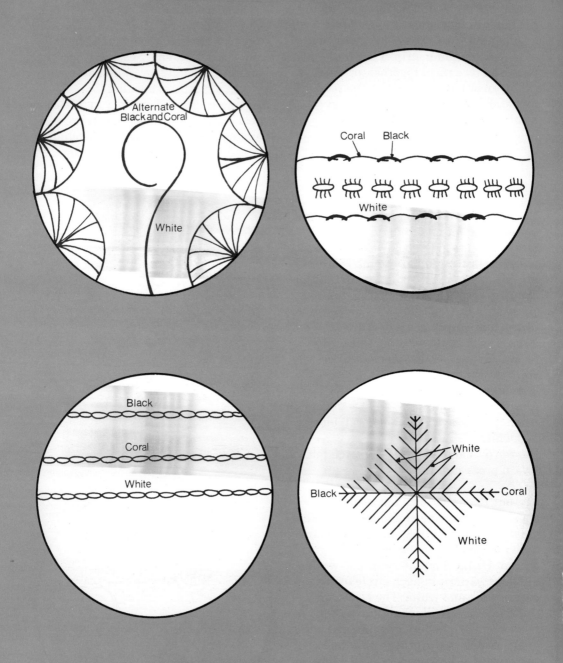

Alternate
Black and Coral

White

Coral   Black

White

Black

Coral

White

White

Black →

← Coral

White

Purse, check cushion

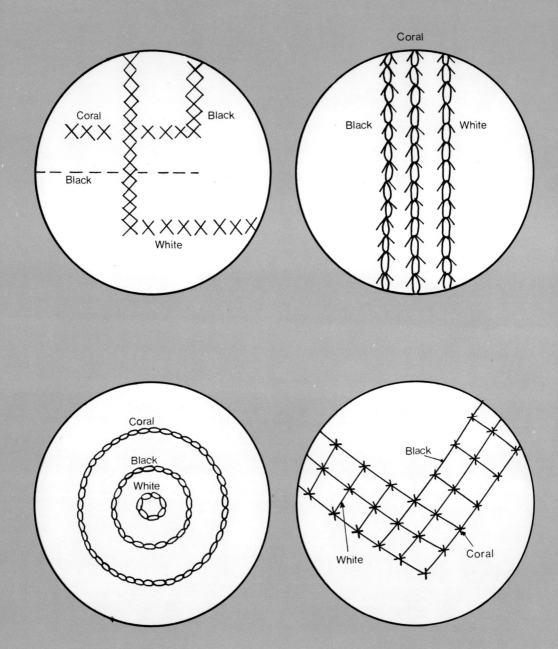

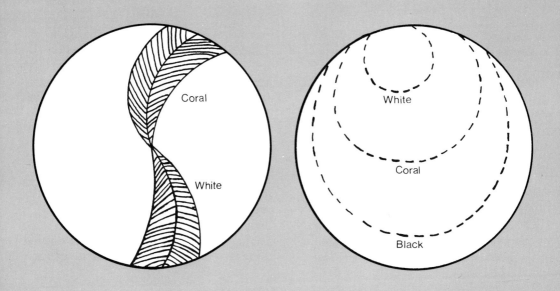

Beadwork

Here are some lovely gifts to make using beads. Small embroidery beads have been used for some and wooden beads for others. The techniques are simple and you will have great fun making pretty and unusual jewellery for your friends. The woven bracelet illustrated was made on a bead loom but you can improvise a loom from a cardboard shoe box or make one from three pieces of wood. Two ways of improvising a loom are illustrated (diagrams 1 and 2).
The instructions for weaving are exactly the same whether you are working on a proper beadloom or a home-made loom.

one more warp thread than there are beads in the pattern and then, to give extra strength to the weaving, there should be one more thread on each side. The *two* outside threads are always used together.

Preparing the loom Cut the warp threads to the length of finished beading required plus 6 inches. (The bracelet has 10 beads across the width, so 13 threads were strung on the loom. The finished length of bracelet is 7 inches so 13 inches of thread would have been needed at least. In fact, beadweaving looms are

Wooden loom

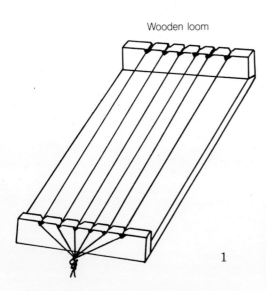

1

Cardboard box loom

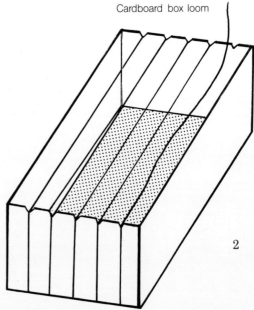

2

The principle of bead weaving The lengthwise threads are called the warp threads and beads lie between them. Therefore the distance between the warp threads must be the same as the size of the bead you are using. Remember this point when cutting the notches on a home-made loom. There must always be

longer than this and it was necessary to cut the threads 20 inches long to allow for stringing up.)
Thread the needle with working thread. Tie the end to the double threads on the left of the loom. (Do not have too long a

114

Choker, woven bracelet, black and yellow necklace, white bead necklace

thread or it will become tangled, about 14 inches is long enough.) Weave four rows without beads to strengthen the weaving. Finish on the left. With the needle, pick up the beads needed for the first row of pattern. (If you are following a set pattern, start counting beads from the left.) Push the beads down on to the thread and place the thread with beads under the warp threads so that a bead lies between each of the warp threads. Press the beads up between the warp threads with a finger of the free hand (diagram 3). Pass the needle from right to left back through the hole in each bead, thus securing them between the warp threads (diagram 4). Pull the thread tight but not too tightly or the straight edge of the weaving will be distorted. Continue in the same way until you have the desired length of beading.

Finishing off Work two or three rows of weaving without beads. Take the working thread back through the last row but one of the weaving. Knot off and cut the thread. Lift the warp threads off the loom. Cut the warp threads to about 3 inches. Tie a loose knot in each thread, and take the thread back through the weaving. Move the knot up to the last row of beads with a pin. This is the method used if a fastening is not being attached to the weaving.

Designs in beadweaving You can work out your own designs for beadweaving on squared paper using coloured felt tipped pens. Simply decide the width of the finished work and the length. Count off the number of squares and colour them in, each square representing one bead. Remember, when following a pattern, the first bead picked up is the bead on the left of your drawn out pattern.

Woven bracelet

illustrated on page 115

Materials
Assorted embroidery beads, seven different tones of blue and green, plus white

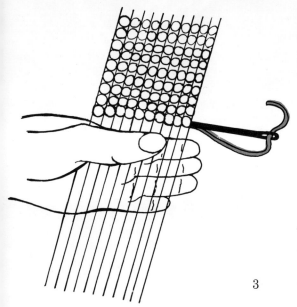

3

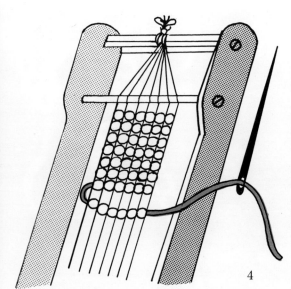

4

Linen beading thread
Beading needle
Bracelet clasp (jeweller's findings)

The bracelet is worked in a random pattern as already described, with ten beads across the width. It is finished off as follows:
Work two rows of weaving without beads. Thread warp threads 2 and 3 back through the beads so that they lie alongside the doubled outside threads. Thread all four threads through five more beads. Do the same with the remaining beads, working in groups.

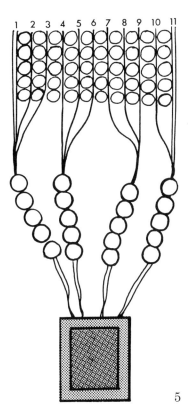

5

Thus, warp threads 1, 2, 3 have five beads on them, 4, 5 and 6 have five beads, 7, 8 and 9 have five beads and 10 and 11 have five beads. Knot the ends to a bracelet fastening, (diagram 5). Work the other end of the bracelet in the same way.

Key ring mascot

illustrated on page 119

Amusing key ring mascots looking like little character dolls can be made very quickly and cheaply, using wooden or plastic beads and wire. Choose beads in colours to dress the doll and paint features on the head bead.
The diagram gives the pattern for threading up the mascot doll.
The mascot is fastened to a bought key ring unit.

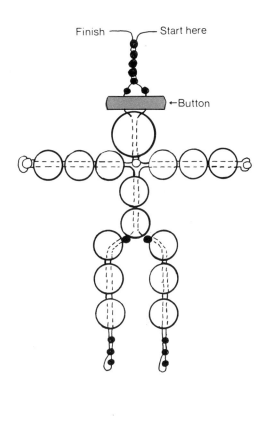

Bead butterfly

illustrated on page 119

The bead butterfly uses a different beadwork technique, that of threading beads on to wire. Silver jeweller's wire is the best but 10 amp fuse wire works just as well.

Materials

Silver wire or fuse wire
Pale blue and silver embroidery beads
Silver baguette beads
Large silver metal bead
Blue and green sequins
Brooch fastening (jeweller's findings)
Epoxy adhesive
Each wing is made in the same way and
the wings are joined in forming the body
and head.

Making a wing Cut 36 inches of wire
and thread two silver beads on to it,
centring them on the wire. This makes
the first row. After this, *both* ends of the
wire are threaded through each row
of beads (diagram 1)
2nd row Thread 1 silver, 1 baguette,
1 silver bead.
3rd row 2 silver, 7 blue, 2 silver.
4th row 2 silver, 11 blue, 2 silver.
From this point, you will be able to
follow diagram 2. Shape the wing as

shown in this diagram until the centre is
reached. Do not cut the wires. Make the
second wing in the same way.
The body is made up of two rows of

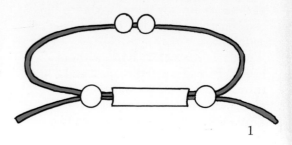

1

silver baguette beads, with a single
silver bead between each. The tail
consists of seven silver beads and the
head is one large metal bead with a
single silver bead on the end of the
twisted wires for antennae.
Glue the brooch fastening to the back
with epoxy adhesive. Attach sequins
with epoxy adhesive.

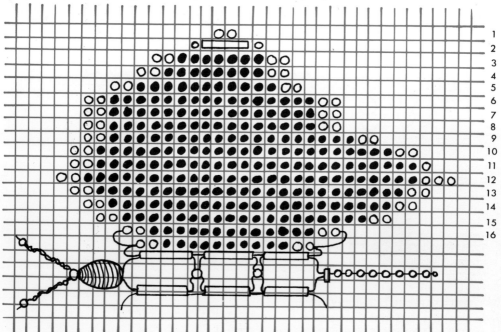

*2. On the final, inside, row of the wing, the right-hand wire links the two body beads to the
three baguette beads. It then goes through the head bead, makes the antennae and is twisted
under the head bead to finish. The left-hand wire goes through the baguettes, into the tail
and is twisted just above the tail to finish.*

*Wooden bead necklace, bead butterfly, key
ring mascot*

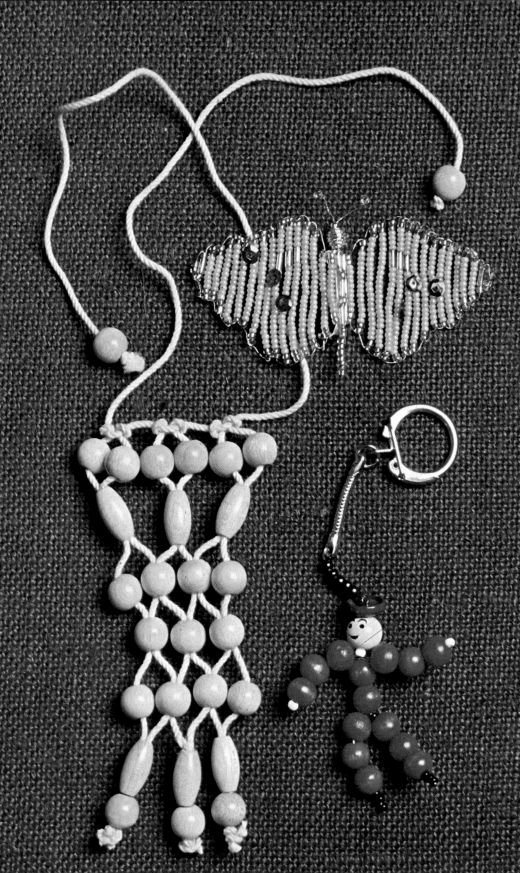

Wooden bead necklace

illustrated on page 119

This necklace uses a different technique: the cords on which the beads are strung are first knotted on to a leader cord. The pattern is achieved by passing the cords through adjacent beads. Soap the ends of the cords to make bead threading easier. Diagram 1 gives the pattern for the necklace illustrated.

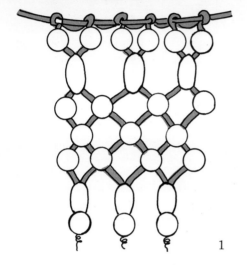

1

Materials
20 round wooden beads
6 long wooden beads
Macramé twine

Cut three lengths of twine, 16 inches long and one length 20 inches long. Double the three lengths and attach them to the long length of twine using the macramé knot (diagram 2).

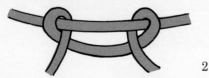

2

String one round bead on each of the six ends. Pass both ends of each pair of cords through a single long bead. The third row has four round beads in

it; bead 1 goes on to cord one; bead 2 is strung on to cords 2 and 3; bead 3 goes on to cords 4 and 5 and the fourth bead goes on to cord 6.
Three round beads make up the next row: cords 1 and 2 go through the first bead; cords 3 and 4 go through the second bead and cords 5 and 6 go through the third bead.
The next row (5) has 4 round beads and the sixth row has the 6 cords passing through three long beads in pairs. One round bead is strung after each long bead and the ends knotted off.
Tie a single round bead on the necklace ends. Knot the ends to fasten the necklace.

White bead necklace

illustrated on page 115

Materials
2 packets small white embroidery beads
Linen beading thread
Necklace fastening (jeweller's findings)
2 beading needles

Cut a length of thread 90 inches long. Thread a needle on both ends. Thread 12 beads on to the thread and centre the beads. Pass both needles

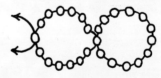

through one more bead. Thread 6 beads on to the left-hand needle and 6 beads on to the right, then pass both needles through one more bead. Continue threading the same way until the necklace is the desired length or until the thread has been covered. Make a loop of 18 beads on one end, taking one end of thread back through the fourth bead and knotting off the thread. Knot a large bead onto the other end of the necklace.

Black and Yellow necklace

illustrated on page 115

Materials
1 packet yellow beads
1 packet black beads
Linen beading thread or nylon thread
2 beading needles

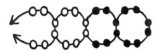

One whole pattern has 12 beads in it,
8 making a complete circle and four
making a half circle. Thread the first
6 beads on 90 inches of thread and pass
both ends through 2 more beads. Thread
2 more beads of the same colour onto
each end of the thread and then cross
the ends through 2 beads of the contrast
colour. Complete the circle in the second
colour with 6 beads, crossing the threads
through the last 2. Proceed in this way
until the necklace is the desired length.
Knot off the ends.

Choker

illustrated on page 115

Materials
1 packet of small beads in each of the
following colours:
scarlet, black, yellow, white
1 packet mixed small beads
4 beading needles
Linen or nylon thread
1 large bead

The choker is made separately from the
single strand attaching ends of the
necklace.
Cut two 90 inch lengths of thread and
put a needle on both ends of each length.
Thread one bead onto each length and
pin the beads to a pincushion or a
beading board.
Follow the diagram for the pattern

using the four ends as indicated. The
necklace illustrated has 3 repeats in
black, 8 in yellow, 3 in black, 8 in
scarlet, 3 in black, 8 in yellow, finishing
with 3 black. Fasten off the four ends by
crossing ends and threading back
through 3 patterns.

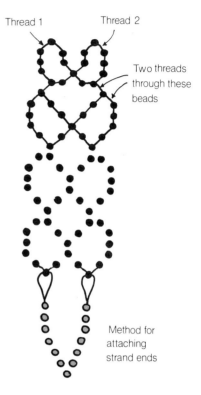

Thread 1   Thread 2

Two threads
through these
beads

Method for
attaching
strand ends

Make the ends
Make the looped end by cutting a 16 inch
length of thread and putting a needle on
each end. Thread 28 beads of mixed
colours on the thread passing both
needles through the last bead to make a
loop. Thread single beads onto both
threads until strand measures 5 inches.
Separate threads. Thread 8 beads onto
each, pass threads through the loops of
the last choker pattern (black) and back
through the 8 beads. Knot off. This
fastens the choker section to the strand
fastening.
Make the other strand fastening in the
same way but begin by threading on a
single large bead.

Candlemaking

Candlemaking is a craft which is open to everyone; hand-made candles are always very acceptable gifts and are sure sellers at fund-raising sales and bazaars.

The basic materials for candle making can be obtained in most large towns and cities and many of the suppliers will supply their goods by post. Moulds, wax, candle colours and wicks are all part of the candlemaker's basic equipment but if you want to make it an almost no-cost craft, old candles can be melted down and wax crayons used for colouring and decoration.

Materials
A large supply of newspaper
Large and small metal containers for melting down wax
Sugar thermometer
Spoons
Sharp knives
Wooden sticks
Paraffin wax
Stearin
Candle colourings
Candlewick
Moulds of different kinds

Paraffin wax Wax for candlemaking is supplied in solid blocks or in powdered form. Both are equally good but the powdered form is easier to use as the blocks have to be shaved down or broken up before melting.

Stearin Stearin is a type of wax which allows wax dyes to dissolve readily and with complete colour suspension. Stearin is not essential but it does produce a more opaque and intense colour and a more durable candle. It also acts as a mould release.

Candlewicks Authentic candlewicking, available from candlemakers' supply shops, is bleached linen thread, woven and graded to burn a certain area of wax without smoking or excessive melting. It is essential to use the right grade of wick in a candle: a wick designated as 1 inch will successfully burn a candle 1 inch in diameter. It will also burn a 1 inch hole in a thicker candle which will result in the wick being drowned in a pool of wax!

If candlewick really is impossible to obtain, you can make candlewicking at home, but it is not quite as satisfactory as the real thing. To make candlewick, use soft cotton string. Cut a length about 12 feet. Dissolve one tablespoon of salt and two tablespoons of borax in one cup of water. Put the string in the solution and let it soak for about 12 hours. Hang to dry out completely. When the string is dry, coat it by dipping in wax and use as directed.

Candle colours Candle wax dyes in powder form and in discs are available from craft shops. A small pinch of powder to a pint of liquid wax is usually enough to achieve a good colour. If the colour is too intense it can spoil the candle's glow.

Wax crayons can be used but experiment first before using them to make sure that you can achieve the effect you want.

Moulds Craft shops sell an exciting selection of ready-made moulds for candlemaking but improvised moulds work very well and produce fascinating shapes. Many kinds of household containers can be used as long as they

Twisted candle, sand candle, jewelled candle, moulded candle, layered candle

are leakproof and do not dissolve under heat of melted wax. Some plastics will do this and it is best to experiment with hot water first. Yoghurt and cream cartons, food cans, cardboard boxes and rubber balls are just a few of the things which can be used but remember that the candle has to be removed when set. The mould must therefore be able to be torn off the candle, or the neck must be large enough for the candle to slip out. Some cartons have a small mouth and a large base, and in this instance, the base can be cut off when the candle has set and the candle removed from this end. If cardboard moulds are used, oil the inside first so that the candle slips out more easily.

Measure out the powdered or broken up wax. Measure out the stearin – 1 part stearin to ten parts of wax. Melt the stearin gently in a saucepan and when dissolved, add the colouring agent. Melt the paraffin wax in a second saucepan and when this has melted, add the stearin colour mixture. Take care not to overheat wax and do not use water near it while it is hot or it will splutter and may cause burns.

The various temperatures for candlemaking are given with the specific instructions.

Moulded candles

Ready-made moulds, made of either latex or metal have no wick holes and these must be pierced with a needle. Dip the wick in wax to protect it then thread the wick through the hole and tie the other end to a wooden stick. Rest this across the top of the mould. Seal the hole and wick with mould seal or clay. (Plasticine will not do as it melts.) Support the mould by hanging it on a rack (diagram 1), which can be improvised by resting two long sticks across two or three bricks, books or flower pots. Heat the wax to 180°F and pour slowly into the mould. Tap the sides to release air bubbles. After a little while, a well will form round the wick as the cooling wax contracts. Prod the surface to break the skin and top up with wax, again heated to 180°F. Do this as often as the well forms. When the wax

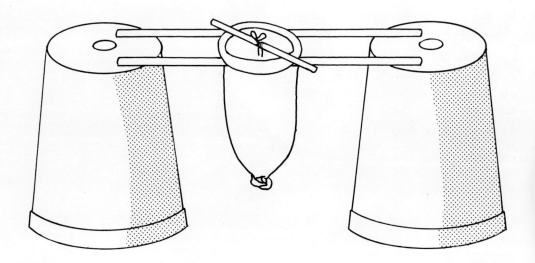

1

has completely hardened, peel back the surface of the mould with soapy hands. (The mould should be washed and dried carefully after use.) Trim the wick and polish the candle in the hands. If the mould is a decorative one, colour can be added by mixing a little water paint with soap. Paint the candle, rubbing some into the crevices of the design and then rub most of the colour off just before it dries. Use water colour sparingly as it does not burn and may clog the wick.

The zigzag candle (illustrated on page 127) is made by first casting 5 yellow, 5 red and 4 turquoise wax discs in an egg poacher. When set, a wick hole is made in the centre of each disc. These are then dropped into a glass mould, one on top of the other so that the curved bases face alternately up and down. Very strongly dyed brown wax, heated to 240°F, is then poured in and the mould shaken to release any trapped air. The candle is then cooled rapidly and finally carved by hand and dipped into hot wax (230°F) to seal and gloss.

Improvised moulds If a simple container such as a soup can is being used as a mould, simply pour the melted wax into the can (180°F). Tie the wick to a stick and balance it across the top of the can. Leave to cool, topping up the well as before. Remove the hardened candle either by removing the bottom of the can and pushing the candle out or dip the can in hot water for a few moments.

For a different effect, make a 'jewelled' candle. Break up pieces of different coloured wax and stick them to the sides of the can with a little melted wax. Pour the wax in little by little, so that it sets round the pieces without melting them; or pieces of coloured wax can be added to a completed candle by dipping the pieces in melted wax and pressing them on the candle sides.

The 'jewelled' yellow and lilac candle (illustrated on page 123) is made by pouring yellow and lilac wax into round ice-cube moulds to half-fill these. When set, these half-spheres are fixed with wax glue to the sides of a white candle. The candle is then dipped into hot wax (230°F) to seal and gloss.

Carved candles

This type of candle involves a dipping technique, the oldest known method of making a candle. Fill a jug with wax heated to 180°F. The jug should be just deeper than the intended length of candle. Tie a short length of wick to a stick and dip it into the wax. Hold it in the air for about 30 seconds and the wax will harden. Dip again and again until the candle is thick enough. If a succession of different colours is used for dipping until each layer is about $\frac{1}{4}$ inch thick, the completed candle can be carved back in some areas to reveal the different colours.

For a simpler surface decoration, try impressing a finished candle with various sharp objects such as nails or screwheads, or small cookie cutters.

Twisted candles

These are made by flattening a dipped candle while still soft with a rolling pin. The flattened strip is held in both hands and gently twisted. The candle is then plunged into cold water to harden.

Layered candles

To make layered candles, have ready a large container of cold water. Pierce the can at the bottom and thread the wick through. Knot it underneath and then seal off with clay. Tie the other end to a stick and rest the stick across the can. Pour a little wax into the bottom of the can and stand it in the cold water, resting the can against the side of the container (diagram 2). As each layer sets, pour in different coloured waxes, layer by layer until the can is filled. (diagram 3)

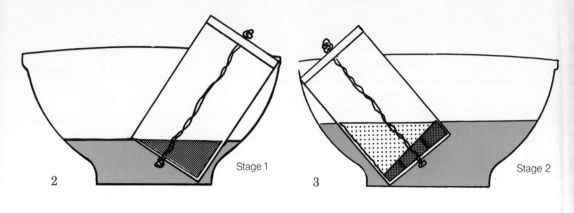

2   Stage 1   3   Stage 2

Sand candles

These are great fun to make and well worth an experiment. Fill a small box

hole. Refill the hole as the level of the wax falls. Allow the candle to harden in a cold place for about 2 hours. Make a hole in the centre with a thin knitting

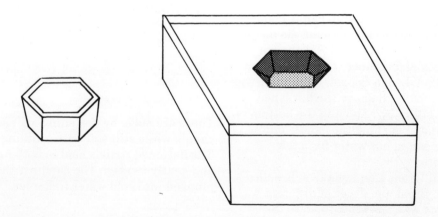

1

with damp sand. Dig a hole and push a small article such as a box, an ashtray, a cup or a bottle, into the sand (diagram 1) to shape the hole as required. Remove the article. Heat the wax to 250°F and pour it carefully into the centre of the

needle and leave it standing in the candle. Leave the candle to harden completely overnight.

Next day, dig the candle out and brush away any loose sand. Remove the needle and insert a wick. Choose a wick which

126

Balloon candle, zig-zag candle, star mould candles

will leave some wax unburned – for instance, if the approximate diameter of the candle is 3 inches, choose a wick which will burn 2 inches. This will ensure that the sand shell remains after the candle has burned away and the shell can be used again. Top up the hole round the wick with melted wax (220°F). You can now carve away areas of sand. Do not carve too deeply or you will carve into the wax itself.